"This unique experientially-focused workbook has fun and engaging reflective activities that are sure to be a help for counselors-in-training as they develop a deeper understanding of their aspirations, identity, role, and path in the counseling profession." – *Mark D. Stauffer, Ph.D., core faculty, Walden University*

"This is a one of a kind resource for educators and students alike. Each chapter provides a solid literature review followed by creative interventions that facilitate a student's journey to becoming a healer. The activities have clear instructions, templates, individual/group processing, and supervision reflection prompts. Each chapter helps programs and students achieve the CACREP Standards that encourage reflection and awareness of Self. I cannot wait to implement this resource in our program!" – *LoriAnn S. Stretch, LPC-S, NCC, ACS, BC-TMH, department chair, The Chicago School of Professional Psychology*

"Resources adopted for use by graduate students new to the profession of counseling must be written in a way that captures the interest and encourages the development of the professional identity of the beginning counselor. This workbook, designed for use in practicum and internship seminars and placements, contains cutting-edge descriptions of reflective and creative activities specifically designed to provide a reflective space to connect knowledge of counseling content and skills to the personal attributes and experiences of the reader. I recommend this workbook without hesitation or reservation." – *David Capuzzi, Ph.D., LPC, NCC, past president, American Counseling Association*

THE REFLECTIVE COUNSELOR

This practical workbook contains 45 experiential and creative activities intentionally created to facilitate counselor professional identity development. Each reflective activity is designed for students and supervisees to learn more about counselor professional identity, as well as integrate their knowledge of counseling skills and content with personal attributes and experiences. Individual and group process questions and group follow-up activities make this an ideal workbook to supplement classes or group supervision. Upon completion of the workbook, students and supervisees will have a journal of their process in the beginning stages of counselor professional identity development. With chapters focusing on areas including counselor wellness, self-growth, personal and professional values, multicultural awareness, research and assessment, and more, *The Reflective Counselor* is an essential resource for counseling graduate students, supervisees, and new professionals alike.

Michelle S. Hinkle, Ph.D. is an associate professor in the Professional Counseling Program at William Paterson University in Wayne, New Jersey. She is a licensed professional counselor and approved clinical supervisor.

Meredith Drew, Ph.D. is an associate professor in the Professional Counseling Program at William Paterson University in Wayne, New Jersey. She is a licensed professional counselor, national certified counselor, certified school counselor, and approved clinical supervisor.

THE REFLECTIVE COUNSELOR

45 Activities for Developing Your Professional Identity

Michelle S. Hinkle and Meredith Drew

Routledge
Taylor & Francis Group

NEW YORK AND LONDON

First published 2020
by Routledge
52 Vanderbilt Avenue, New York, NY 10017

and by Routledge
2 Park Square, Milton Park, Abingdon, Oxon, OX14 4RN

Routledge is an imprint of the Taylor & Francis Group, an informa business

Library of Congress Cataloging-in-Publication Data
Names: Hinkle, Michelle S., author. | Drew, Meredith, author.
Title: The reflective counselor : 45 activities for developing your
    professional identity / Michelle S. Hinkle and Meredith Drew.
Description: New York, NY : Routledge, 2020. | Includes bibliographical
    references and index. |
Identifiers: LCCN 2019043689 (print) | LCCN 2019043690 (ebook) | ISBN
    9780367182960 (hbk) | ISBN 9780367182977 (pbk) | ISBN
    9780429203657 (ebk)
Subjects: LCSH: Counselors—Professional ethics.
Classification: LCC BF636.67 .H56 2020 (print) | LCC BF636.67 (ebook) |
    DDC 158.3023—dc23
LC record available at https://lccn.loc.gov/2019043689
LC ebook record available at https://lccn.loc.gov/2019043690

ISBN: 978-0-367-18296-0 (hbk)
ISBN: 978-0-367-18297-7 (pbk)
ISBN: 978-0-429-20365-7 (ebk)

Typeset in Stone Serif
by Swales & Willis, Exeter, Devon, UK

To all emerging counselors, may you strive for professional identity and find your mark on the counseling field.

CONTENTS

Acknowledgments   xii
Author Biographies   xiii
Preface   xiv

CHAPTER 1   **Professional Identity as a Shared and Integrated Philosophy of Professional Counseling**   1

Connecting Professional Identity to You   2

Activity 1: Though Art Almost a Counselor   3

Activity 2: Gift Giving   9

Activity 3: Sharing the View   15

Activity 4: The Game of Counseling   21

CHAPTER 2   **Self-Exploration**   28

Connecting Self-Exploration to You   29

Activity 5: Roots to Sky   31

Activity 6: Put a Pin in It   37

Activity 7: My Emerging Self   43

Activity 8: Personal Philosophies   49

CHAPTER 3   **Counselor Wellness**   56

Connecting Wellness to You   58

Activity 9: Color My Heart   59

Activity 10: Framing It Out   65

Activity 11: Identifying Success and Finding Your Place   71

Activity 12: Self-Care That Fits For You   77

CHAPTER 4   **Ethics and Counseling**   **84**

Connecting Ethics to You   85

Activity 13: Ethics Cartoons   87

Activity 14: Symbolism   93

Activity 15: Superhero Alter Ego   99

Activity 16: Center of You   105

CHAPTER 5   **Multicultural Awareness**   **112**

Connecting Multicultural Awareness to You   114

Activity 17: The Hidden Self   115

Activity 18: My Cultural Self   121

Activity 19: The Body   127

Activity 20: Sending Greetings from a New View   133

CHAPTER 6   **Theoretical Orientation**   **140**

Connecting Theoretical Orientation to You   142

Activity 21: Theory Road Map   143

Activity 22: Metaphor for Change   149

Activity 23: Theory Fill-in-the-Blank   155

Activity 24: The Theory of You   161

CHAPTER 7   **Personal and Professional Values**   **168**

Connecting Personal and Professional Values to You   169

Activity 25: Connect Your Values   171

Activity 26: Celebrity Role Model   177

Activity 27: ABCs & 123s   183

Activity 28: Parts Picnic   189

CHAPTER 8   **Building Community Through Credentials and Professional Organizations**   **196**

Connecting Credentials and Professional Organizations to You   198

Activity 29: Credentials: Alphabet Soup after Your Name   199

Activity 30: Billboard Advertisement   205

Activity 31: Vision Board   211

Activity 32: Advocating for Counseling   217

CHAPTER 9   **Career Exploration**   **224**

Connecting Career Exploration to You   225

Activity 33: Career Jar   227

Activity 34: Elevator Speech   233

Activity 35: Supporting Roles   239

Activity 36: Current Issues and Breaking News   245

CHAPTER 10   **Research and Assessment**   **252**

Connecting Research and Assessment to You   253

Activity 37: Research Your Needs   255

Activity 38: Case Study Reflection   261

Activity 39: Job Assessment   267

Activity 40: Show and Tell   273

CHAPTER 11   **Self-Growth and the Future**   **280**

Connecting Self-Growth and the Future to You   281

Activity 41: #PlayHardBeSmartHaveFun   283

Activity 42: To Whom It May Concern   289

Activity 43: Color Code Your Future   295

Activity 44: Then, Now, Soon   301

Epilogue   308

Activity 45: Termination Farewell Dinner   311

Reflections from Group Members   317

Bonus Activity: Your Counselor Professional Identity Statement   318

ACKNOWLEDGMENTS

The contents of this workbook would not be possible without the efforts of leaders and researchers in the professional counseling field. We appreciate the work, dedication, and leadership of the mentors we have known personally, as well as those who we have never met but exemplify strong professional identity and strengthen our field further. We thank our former professors and supervisors who not only taught us how to be counselors and counselor educators, but also challenged us in our own professional identity development. We value professional relationships we have had with peers and colleagues, including our faculty at William Paterson University. Our professional community continues to influence the expression of our own professional identity.

The students and supervisees we have worked with over the years challenge us to be better counselor educators and supervisors, and we are grateful they inspired the ideas contained in this workbook. We would like to acknowledge the research support of our Graduate Assistant, Kelly Mabin, from the William Paterson University Professional Counseling Program. Her assistance to our project was greatly appreciated.

Finally, we extend love and appreciation to our families. To our husbands, Jeff and Adam, thank you for your ongoing support and encouragement as we completed this book. To our children, Paul and Ben, and Joseph, Nicolas, and Ava, thank you for your patience and understanding and reminding us to take breaks for play and fun.

AUTHOR BIOGRAPHIES

Michelle S. Hinkle, PhD, LPC, ACS is an Associate Professor in the Professional Counseling Program at William Paterson University in Wayne, NJ. In this capacity, she teaches a variety of counselor education courses and supervises counselor trainees and currently serves as a faculty advisor for Chi Sigma Iota (CSI). She holds a master's degree in Counseling and a doctorate in Counselor Education and Supervision and is a Licensed Professional Counselor and Approved Clinical Supervisor. Dr. Hinkle's clinical experience is in mental health counseling. The majority of that clinical work was with children, adolescents, and families where she used strength-based counseling theories and interventions to help clients achieve their goals. Dr. Hinkle's scholarly interests include counselor education, strength-based counseling and supervision, and using creativity in counseling, supervision, and teaching. She has co-authored book chapters and articles in counseling journals related to her interest areas, as well as presented at conferences. Dr. Hinkle holds active membership in ACA and ACC. She is also a member of CSI, ACES, and NARACES, all in which she has provided service or held leadership positions.

Meredith Drew, PhD, LPC, NCC, ACS is an Associate Professor in the Professional Counseling Program at William Paterson University in Wayne, NJ. In this capacity, she teaches a variety of counselor education courses and supervises counselor trainees. She holds a master's degree in Education with a concentration in Counseling and a doctorate in Counselor Education and Supervision and is a Licensed Professional Counselor, National Certified Counselor, Approved Clinical Supervisor, and Certified School Counselor. Dr. Drew's clinical experience is in mental health counseling and school counseling, having spent many years working with children and adolescents in both settings. Dr. Drew's scholarly interests include counselor education, supervision, school counseling, wellness/self-care, and using creativity in counseling, supervision, and teaching. She has co-authored book chapters and articles in counseling journals related to her interest areas. She has presented internationally, nationally, regionally, and state-wide on topics related to her interest areas. Dr. Drew received Teacher of the Year award for exemplary teaching and was an Emerging Leader Award recipient at ACES. Dr. Drew holds active membership in ACA, ACC, CSI, and she has had the opportunity to hold leadership and service positions in ACES, NARACES, and is Past President of NJACES.

PREFACE

Before I (Michelle) began graduate school I knew I wanted to be a "helper." I imagined myself sitting in a future office listening to people describe their lives, problems, or dreams and facilitating their process of resolution and growth. This was the extent of my fantasy. I did not know how to help the people who came to my pretend office or the steps I would take in helping them find their full potential. I also never had an image of the business cards (surely kept in my imaginary desk drawer) so I did not even know the credentials that equipped me to work. All I knew is that I needed to go to graduate school. But where would I go and for what degree?

I applied to my master's of counseling program not knowing the difference between counseling, social work, psychology, and other helping professions. All I knew at the time was that the program's website seemed to indicate that upon graduation I could make my aspirations come true. That, along with the application essay prompt asking me why I wanted to be a counselor and the warm and inviting interview process, upon which I left in awe at the professors' questions that magically made it easy to talk, made my decision that I would enroll if accepted.

I was accepted, and I loved every minute of my education. From the moment I began my studies, I knew that I had found a professional home. I loved the theories and skills I was learning and practicing in all of my courses, and class discussions left me wanting more. I knew I made the right choice in attending a counseling program and that embarking on a future as a professional counselor was a perfect fit for me. It just *felt* right but at the time I could not articulate how or why it was the best choice for me. What I learned much later was that the philosophical tenets of counseling aligned and worked well with many of my personal values, as well as my motivations in wanting to be a counselor in the first place. Additionally, the skills and theories I was learning, and the ones I eventually gravitated to, were authentic with my personality and attributes. Being able to eventually identify this was useful in my counselor professional identity process but took time and reflection on both my personal and professional selves.

Though I had an excellent education and was confident in my abilities upon graduation, when I was a new counselor I still stumbled when others referred to me as a social worker, family therapist, or psychologist. I knew I needed to correct them but did not always feel confident in my ability to describe the difference among all these helping professions. Don't all of these professionals work with people to help them resolve problems or overcome obstacles? Aside from my degree and title, what was the difference? I became starkly aware of the importance in clearly defining professions and job roles during an experience in my doctoral studies. When reviewing my CV, one of my professors remarked on my use of "counselor" as a professional title previous to my earning a master's degree and license in counseling. My job title at the group home where I previously worked was, in fact, "counselor" but it made me aware that using the term before earning the proper distinctions can minimize the professional title. After all, there are camp counselors, counselors at law, genetic counselors, and more jobs that use the word. I suddenly became aware of the vital need to advocate for professional counseling as a distinct profession separate from other helping fields, as well as from other job titles of "counselor."

Through my education, counseling work, and experiences, my professional identity has evolved over time. I can now confidently and proudly describe professional counseling as a distinct discipline. I can also describe exactly why it is my professional home. I have had wonderful opportunities of professional identity expression by finding ways to contribute to professional organizations, attending conferences, extending my credentials, and learning more about professional interest areas through workshops and continuing education. I have also paid attention to those around me and observed how leaders in our field express their professional identity and advocate for professional counseling. Further, my conversations with colleagues and the things I've learned from them, as well as from former professors, supervisors, clients, supervisees, and students, have helped me continually construct and define my counselor professional identity.

My (Meredith) journey towards becoming a counselor began in high school with that first psychology class and continued through college. I knew I would attend graduate school to enable me to reach my goals, but I felt overwhelmed by the many professional choices that my dreams towards "helping" involved. I found a mentor early on that helped tremendously to get me to the place where I truly feel at home as a counselor educator. Much like Michelle, early in my development I was often confused by the differences between social workers, psychologists, and other helpers but also knew that I truly enjoyed my counseling courses. These courses were different than those of friends I had in social work programs. My classes focused on theory, interventions, techniques, and I had classes that allowed for concentrated time to practice skills. These classes were key for me to connect to my role as a counselor. But I still struggled to clearly identify who I was as a professional. I wish I had more time in my graduate program to really reflect on my personal being and my newly created professional being. The process of understanding the relationship between the two is so crucial and I believe has made me a better counselor.

This eventually happened for me as I continued on my journey to complete my master's degree and began supervision of my hours towards my license. My supervisor really helped me to clearly define who I was and how I viewed my clients. My supervisor was able to take the book content and apply it to my cases and help me to see what I already connected to, but did not realize. Through our supervisory relationship and processing of my own responses to clients and experiences, she was able to help me define what was most important to me in my own professional identity. I had already felt like I was home when I began in the counseling field, but my work with my supervisor made me feel like I owned my home. That was such a crucial moment because I became confident as a counselor and that confidence led to greater presence with my clients, more authenticity in client relationships, and a stronger sense of who I am as a counselor. These moments were critical for me, and I believe this really was the springboard when I fully felt like I had earned the title of "professional counselor."

The professional identity I hold has changed slightly from my early days, but it has only expanded to add new roles that I have been lucky to hold. The privilege of being a counselor is one that I try not to take for granted. The helping role of a counselor is so much bigger than that simple word, and yet I struggle to find a better word to express it. As a counselor, we are all able to help our clients in a million different ways. That is a gift to our clients, but also a gift we give to ourselves each day.

If you were to ask any of your professors, supervisors, or other professional counseling colleagues about momentous experiences in their counselor professional identity development, they would likely be able to describe a time that was impactful. It could range from the feeling of belonging at their first professional conference, or pride the day when they opened the mail to find their long-awaited and hard-earned state license or credential. Perhaps it was a feeling of recognition when they received a thank you note from a client, satisfaction in describing professional competencies to a superior, or gratitude when they opened a counseling journal and saw an article that provided resources for a clinical struggle. Regardless, there are many occasions that could elicit a connectedness to the profession and appreciation for being a professional counselor.

As counselor educators, we continually share ideas and discuss the strategies we use to help students and supervisees begin their own counselor professional identity development. We want emerging, and new, counselors to easily articulate how professional counseling is a distinct helping field, what it means to be a professional counselor, and how it is the right career path for them. Just like we have always known that being a professional counselor was perfect for our attributes, beliefs, and values, we want to help students find a sense of fit with the profession by identifying how being a professional counselor was the right choice for them and how they experience a *good fit* with the profession.

These ideas and conversations provided the foundation for this workbook. The activities within are aimed to help you enhance your developing counselor professional identity. We offer ways to explore the counseling field and provide opportunities to personally connect with the counseling competencies you have learned in your studies. By the end of the book, we want you to confidently, clearly, and concisely communicate the foundation of professional counseling as a distinct helping profession. Further, we want you to find your connection to the field as to describe how you uniquely find belonging in the field and express yourself through your counselor professional identity. Ultimately, through the activities in this book, you will find ways to incorporate your personal identity into your counselor professional identity expression.

Introduction to Counselor Professional Identity

Developing professional identity is something that all counselors are encouraged to do because it strengthens the discipline of counseling (Kaplan & Gladding, 2011; McLaughlin & Boettcher, 2009) and improves counselors' identification with the profession, enhances clinical work, and impacts longevity in the career (Woo, Henfield, & Choi, 2014). Built on intrapersonal and interpersonal levels, a counselor professional identity is two-fold (Gibson, Dollarhide, & Moss, 2010). First, the intrapersonal level, is the culmination of counselors' personal characteristics with their counseling attributes, such as skills, ethics, and decision-making processes (Auxier, Hughes, & Kline, 2003; Gibson et al., 2010; Moss, Gibson, & Dollarhide, 2014; Prosek & Hurt, 2014). This synthesis of attributes between the self and the profession begins in training and supervision as students and new counselors strengthen their abilities and become more confident and independent in their work (Moss et al., 2014). By the time they are in internship, counselor trainees have a better understanding of the profession, as well as their personal values and the potential for their involvement (Gibson et al., 2010; Prosek & Hurt, 2014). This makes practicum, internship, and early career supervision an ideal time for counselor trainees and new counselors to look deeper into their professional identity development.

We intentionally centered this workbook on the practicum and internship portions of your education, or other early supervision experiences post-graduation. By now in your development, you have learned the necessary content and competencies that go into being a professional counselor. You already understand the various elements that go into the role and you now have the opportunity to integrate the concepts and skills you have learned into action at your practicum, internship, or work site. You also have the opportunity to find a counseling style that suits you. This is where that intrapersonal level of counselor professional identity development becomes relevant (Gibson et al., 2010). At this time, you have the chance to use counseling skills and concepts in ways that intertwine your personal attributes and styles. For example, are you naturally comfortable with silence, creative, observant? Do you easily find strengths; do you enjoy group work; do you lean toward cognitions or emotions? Is your style more concrete or abstract? How will you blend these personal traits and beliefs with the skills required of you as a counselor? This process will help you to be a more authentic counselor.

The second part of counseling professional identity consists of holding a shared philosophy and vision of the discipline with other professional counselors (Kaplan & Gladding, 2011). Mellin, Hunt, and Nichols (2011) identified this shared philosophy as one focused on wellness, development, and prevention. Building this interpersonal side of professional identity comes from immersing oneself, and being indoctrinated, into the discipline through supervision, mentorship, licensure, certification, and membership in professional organizations such as the American Counseling Association and Chi Sigma Iota (Dollarhide & Miller, 2006; Gibson et al., 2010). As a practicum or internship supervisee, or new counselor supervisee, you have opportunities to take part in professional development activities while being immersed in a community of other professional counselors. This affords you possibilities to seek mentorship, ask questions, participate in professional development opportunities, attend conferences and activities sponsored by counseling organizations, and observe others' professional identities. This is an exciting time to soak up all of the information around you and start learning about the greater professional counseling community.

The Purpose of This Workbook

On becoming a counselor, Dr. Samuel Gladding said, "You must be a person who knows the depth of his soul and the width of the world. You need to go inside as you go outside" (2009, pp. 33-34). This reflexivity, as Dr. Gladding suggests, is an important process in ongoing professional identity development (Rønnestad & Skovholt, 2003). As a result, the activities in this workbook were specifically designed to provide you with a reflective space. Each one attempts to connect your knowledge of counseling content and skills to your personal attributes and experiences in an attempt to further build your counselor professional identity. Activities are aimed at helping you integrate personal traits with counseling characteristics and embrace a shared philosophy and vision of counseling. We hope to challenge you to think deeper and understand yourself a bit more and strengthen your participation in the professional community.

There are a total of 45 activities in this book, covering 11 important topics in the counseling field. The topics were chosen as they reflect key components of professional identity, CACREP (2016) competency areas for counselors, and topics included within the ACA Code of Ethics (2014). Each chapter has four related activities that we intentionally designed to be experiential and creative in order to enhance awareness to experiences and growth toward building the intra- and interpersonal aspects of professional identity (Gibson et al., 2010). Each activity increases in intensity to challenge your development towards becoming a professional counselor. Because reflection is an important component in professional identity development (Gladding, 2009; Moss et al., 2014; Owens & Neale-McFall, 2014), we also offer open-ended questions to process the activities.

Though the main activities throughout this workbook are to be done individually, we purposefully incorporated group process questions and activities that your class or supervision group can complete together. We believe that conversation, peer support, and community are important components in building counselor professional identity. Therefore, we have included discussion prompts about the individual activities and follow-up activities on related topics so that you can hear multiple perspectives and strength-based feedback, as well as having opportunities to teach, and learn from, peers.

The Structure of This Workbook

Chapter Introductions

Each activity in this workbook has been informed by current research and literature; thus, each chapter begins with an introduction on the related topic. These introductions define the chapter topic, relate the topic to overall counselor professional identity, and provide you with a brief literature review on related information. The introductions end with the connection between the topic and the activities in the chapter. The references in the back of the chapter informed the introduction section, but you can also use the list as resources for further reading on each topic.

The Activity

Each activity in this book is an individual activity for you to complete on your own. The activities require you to think outside the box, get creative, or dig deeper into emotions, cognitions, and experiences. There is space provided to complete the activity or provide evidence of having done so. This is intentional as it helps you manage and organize efforts by providing the space for work and to easily bring the assignment to your supervision group. Further, by keeping work in the space provided, you are able to keep this workbook as a journal. By having reflections all in one place, you can keep track of your growth at the end of the semester, revisit this workbook after graduation to see all that you have accomplished, and look back years from now to remind yourself where you began your counseling career and reconnect with some of those initial feelings and experiences.

Processing Individually

After completing each activity, there are process questions to help you delve further into your experience and emotions in completing the task. In this section, there is space provided for you to reflect upon experiences, make connections between the activity and counseling, and gain insights into your counselor professional identity development. You should be honest with yourself when answering these questions and take note of any additional thoughts or feelings that arise while doing the activity. You should also be aware of anything that is particularly difficult to answer or complete. After individual reflection, any insights, difficulty, or remaining questions about the activity or process might be good topics to discuss in supervision with your supervisor and peers. As you work on the activities, the content and ideas will be fresh in your mind and part of your conscious awareness. There is also a box labeled with a magnifying glass for you to jot down any time you notice concepts playing out around you in your personal life, at your counseling site, in your supervision group, or anywhere else.

Taking It to the Group

Group processing questions are also included with each activity. These questions and prompts are aimed to enhance conversation about the activity, and related topics, by group members so that everyone can learn from each other. This is an opportunity to hear ideas from your peers and expand your own thoughts and perspectives on certain topics. Use this time to ask more questions, learn from others' experiences, and consider how community and conversation can help build your counselor professional identity development.

Follow-Up Group Supervision Activities

This section includes ideas that supervisors and professors might choose to incorporate into group supervision time to expand on the activity topic. The activities provided range from something that takes little time (e.g., a five-minute check-in about a topic) to something that requires forethought and planning (e.g., inviting in a panel of counselors to interview). Regardless, the tasks offered can add to group supervision time and provide follow-up to the main activity.

Additional Thoughts and Supervisor Notes

Each activity contains space to provide your additional thoughts or feelings about the activity. This can also be used for you to take note of any further questions or ideas that arise from your participation in the activity, processing, or the group conversation. You might use this area to indicate your feelings about certain topics or thoughts that persist as you are working, sharing, or listening to others. There is also a box for supervisor notes. This area can be used for you to take notes on your supervisor's feedback or ideas. Alternatively, your supervisor might collect your workbook and use that space to write notes or comments to you.

Constructing Your Counselor Professional Identity

Constructing counselor professional identity is an ongoing and intentional process that can come from reflecting, conversing, observing, and experiencing. We hope you are honest and thorough as you complete the workbook activities and use the questions to reflect on your experiences. Be sure to participate in conversations with your peers about the chapter and activity topics as to share your ideas, provide and get feedback, and hear varying opinions and perspectives. Learn from each other as you hear and observe your peers and your supervisor(s) discussing ideas and engaging in the activities. Take time to be mindful of where and how you see the content within each chapter play out before you at your counseling sites, classrooms, or other professional environments and events. Observe how other, more experienced counselors are exemplifying some of the topics you will experience, write about, or learn in this workbook, and ask questions. Be intentional about trying new ideas or taking note of how you are more aware of, and demonstrating, your counselor professional identity. Finally, have fun exploring and constructing your counselor professional identity.

References

American Counseling Association. (2014). *ACA code of ethics*. Retrieved from www.counseling.org.

Auxier, C. R., Hughes, F. R., & Kline, W. B. (2003). Identity development in counselors-in-training. *Counselor Education and Supervision, 43*, 25–38. doi:10.1002/j.1556-6978.2003.tb01827.x

Council for Accreditation of Counseling and Related Educational Programs. (2016). *CACREP accreditation standards and procedures manual*. Alexandria, VA: Author.

Dollarhide, C. T., & Miller, G. M. (2006). Supervision for preparation and practice of school counselors: Pathways to excellence. *Counselor Education and Supervision, 45*, 242–252. doi:10.1002/j.1556-6978.2006.tb00001.x

Gibson, D. M., Dollarhide, C. T., & Moss, J. M. (2010). Professional identity development: A grounded theory of transformational tasks of new counselors. *Counselor Education and Supervision, 50*, 21–38. doi:10.1002/j.1556-6676.2014.00124.x

Gladding, S. T. (2009). *Becoming a counselor: The light, the bright, and the serious* (2nd ed.). Alexandria, VA: American Counseling Association.

Kaplan, D. M., & Gladding, S. T. (2011). A vision for the future of counseling: The 20/20 Principals for unifying and strengthening the profession. *Journal of Counseling & Development, 89*, 367–372. doi:10.1002/j.1556-6678.2011.tb00101.x

McLaughlin, J. E., & Boettcher, K. (2009). Counselor identity: Conformity or distinction? *Journal of Humanistic Counseling, Education and Development, 48*, 132–143. doi:10.1002/j.2161-1939.2009.tb00074.x

Mellin, E. A., Hunt, B., & Nichols, L. M. (2011). Counselor professional identity: Findings and implications for counseling and interprofessional collaboration. *Journal of Counseling & Development, 89*, 140–147. doi: 10.1002/j.1556-6678.2011.tb00071.x

Moss, J. M., Gibson, D. M., & Dollarhide, C. T. (2014). Professional identity development: A grounded theory of transformational tasks of counselors. *Journal of Counseling & Development, 92*, 3-12. doi:10.1002/j.1556-6676.2014.00124.x

Owens, E. W., & Neale-McFall, C. (2014). Counselor identity development: Toward a model for the formation of professional identity. *Journal of Counselor Leadership and Advocacy, 1*, 16–27. doi:10.1080/2326716X.2014.886975

Prosek, E. A., & Hurt, K. M. (2014). Measuring professional identity development among counselor trainees. *Counselor Education and Supervision, 53*, 284–293. doi:10.1002/j.1556-6978.2014.00063.x

Rønnestad, M. H., & Skovholt, T. M. (2003). The journey of the counselor and therapist: Research findings and perspectives on professional development. *Journal of Career Development, 30*(1), 5–44. doi:10.1023/A:1025173508081

Woo, H., Henfield, M. S., & Choi, N. (2014). Defining professional identity in counseling: A review of the literature. *The Journal of Counselor Leadership & Advocacy, 1*, 1–15. doi:10.1080/23267167X.2014.895452

CHAPTER 1

PROFESSIONAL IDENTITY AS A SHARED AND INTEGRATED PHILOSOPHY OF PROFESSIONAL COUNSELING

At the 2010 American Counseling Association (ACA) national conference, delegates representing various counseling constituencies voted and approved the following definition of the counseling process: "Counseling is a professional relationship that empowers diverse individuals, families, and groups to accomplish mental health, wellness, education, and career goals" (Kaplan, Tarvydas, & Gladding, 2014, p. 368). This definition, endorsed by 29 of 31 ACA participating organizations (Kaplan et al., 2014), was the outcome from *2020: A Vision for the Future of Counseling*. This 20/20 initiative stressed the need to strengthen the identity, and promote recognition, of counseling (Kaplan & Gladding, 2011). Creating this unified definition was an important step in legitimizing professional counseling as a distinct mental health discipline (Calley & Hawley, 2008) and provided a firmer foundation for counseling professional identity. Having a unified professional identity also aids in Medicare reimbursement, 3rd party insurance partnerships, and establishing licensure portability (Reiner, Dobmeier, & Hernández, 2013), as well as longevity as a distinct profession (Woo, Henfield, & Choi, 2014).

In addition to a unified counseling identity as a profession, building a unique professional identity is an essential and important part of being a counselor. Brott and Myers (1999) indicated that professional identity provides a cognitive context and structure for counselors to perform their tasks and responsibilities. Upholding a unified counseling philosophy that is endorsed within the profession, and of which new counselors are indoctrinated, undergirds professional identity. This philosophy is a summation of values and beliefs that are unique to counselors that inform their professional activities and responsibilities and helps them define their role among other mental health professionals (Calley & Hawley, 2008). This unified professional identity is useful for many reasons.

In an effort to define counseling and its associated tasks, Mellin, Hunt, and Nichols (2011) asked professional counselors how they distinguished themselves from psychologists and social workers. Participants in this study endorsed a unified professional identity built upon their specialized training and credentialing specific to counseling and identified a distinct focus on developmental, wellness, and prevention in their work with clients. Remley and Herlihy (2020) further embraced and expanded these distinct areas of focus for counseling by identifying the following philosophical tenets that counselors share when working with clients to resolve mental health issues: (a) using a wellness model of mental health is the best perspective to assist individuals, (b) as most issues and problems are developmental, understanding human growth and development is essential, (c) prevention and early intervention are superior to remediation, and (d) the goal of counseling is to empower clients and client systems to resolve their own problems and teach them to identify and resolve problems autonomously in the future (pp. 27–28). These assumptions, along with the approved definition of counseling, establish the foundation for the counseling profession.

Though knowing and working from the definition and philosophy of counseling are integral aspects of having a counselor professional identity, it is a multi-faceted and complex concept that includes other factors. Over recent years, researchers have studied counselor professional identity to identify its components. Woo and Henfield (2015) created the Professional Identity Scale in Counseling, which isolated six domains that construct counselor professional identity, including: (a) knowledge of the profession, (b) articulation of the philosophy of counseling, (c) established expertise required as a counselor and understanding of professional roles, (d) validate attitudes toward the profession and oneself, (e) be engaged in associated professional behaviors, and (f) interaction with other professionals in the field (p. 96).

Others scholars studying counselor professional identity have indicated that it includes not only an adoption of the shared counseling philosophy and specific training, but also an integration of personal attributes and beliefs with those of the profession (Auxier, Hughes, & Kline, 2003). Nugent and Jones (2009) concluded that counselor professional identity is a culmination of education and training, as well as personal traits that are demonstrated within a professional environment. This requires counselors to consider how personal attributes inform professional activities (Burkholder, 2012) and assess how their values exhibit a "goodness of fit" with those of the profession (Woo, Storlie, & Baltrinic, 2016, p. 285).

In sum, developing a strong counseling professional identity is both an interpersonal and intrapersonal process (Gibson, Dollarhide, & Moss, 2010) that begins in counselor training and continues to develop and strengthen with experience (Moss, Gibson, & Dollarhide, 2014; Prosek & Hurt, 2014; Woo, Lu, Harris, & Cauley, 2017). It requires counselors to be indoctrinated within a shared community of counseling via mentorship, supervision, and participation in professional organizations. Endorsing the shared definition and philosophies of counseling consistent with training, licensure, and credentialing is essential to obtaining professional identity. Further, self-reflection is important in order to know how personal attributes and traits fit with that of professional counseling and work to inform counselors' unique expression of professional identity. Being able to articulate a specific counselor professional identity, which reflects the unified professional identity and unique attributes of the counselor, is useful to ensure ethical practices by staying within related roles and competencies (Ponton & Duba, 2009; Woo et al., 2014) and communicating job roles, skills, and functions to potential employers (Burns, 2017).

Connecting Professional Identity to You

In this chapter, activities are aimed at helping you explore the unified counseling professional identity and begin the integration process between the shared philosophy and definition with your personal beliefs and attributes. You will be asked to consider the unique definition and philosophy of counseling that distinguishes it from other helping professions (e.g., psychology, social work). By researching the foundations of professional counseling, you will be able to clearly articulate what counseling is and what counselors do to promote health and well-being for clients and the community. Further, there will be an opportunity for you to consider how your unique attributes and traits fit and overlap with that of the profession. You will also be encouraged to examine professional boundaries and aspects of your persona that are not integrated or demonstrated when in the counselor role. These tasks will help you begin to integrate your own beliefs and skills with that of the profession in an effort to begin your own counselor professional identity development. Each activity was created in an effort to help you learn more about the foundation of counseling professional identity and be able to articulate and discuss it with others, as well as integrate your own thoughts, beliefs, and traits into the profession.

Activity 1: Though Art Almost a Counselor

Directions: Research professional counseling to determine the shared philosophy and definition of counseling, as well as the contributing factors that distinguish counseling from other helping disciplines. Consider the communal values of the profession, differentiating features, professional organizations, and the unique license. From your research, create an acrostic poem, in which the starting letters of each line spell *Professional Counseling*.

P

R   **C**

O   **O**

F   **U**

E   **N**

S   **S**

S   **E**

I   **L**

O   **I**

N   **N**

A   **G**

L

Processing: Though Art Almost a Counselor

Summarize your poem in one sentence.

_____

_____

_____

_____

Describe your _thoughts_ and _feelings_ about being immersed in professional counseling literature and writing your acrostic poem.

Thoughts:

_____

_____

_____

_____

Feelings:

_____

_____

_____

_____

In what ways did you observe concepts included in your poem this week?

In what ways are your ideas about what it means to be a professional counselor reflected in your poem? What new ideas about professional counseling emerged?

_____

_____

_____

_____

_____

_____

What are ways that counseling distinguishes itself from other helping professions?

_____

_____

_____

_____

_____

_____

Based on what you have learned in your research and writing your poem, write a description of professional counseling that you could share with someone who is unfamiliar with the field.

_____

_____

_____

_____

_____

Taking It to the Group

- How do themes found among group members' poems create a larger picture of counselor professional identity?

- What did group members learn about professional counseling during their research that was surprising?

- What did group members confirm in their knowledge about professional counseling during their research?

- What steps can the group take in order to continue counselor professional identity exploration both as individuals and as a group?

- What makes identifying a professional identity, or a shared vision of counseling, important for counseling advocacy efforts?

My additional thoughts and feelings about the
Though Art Almost A Counselor **activity...**

Supervisor Reflections

Follow-up Supervision Group Activities

- Create a book of each group member's acrostic poem to keep and review throughout supervision. Leave some blank pages to capture any differences or changes to the poems over the course of the group's time together.

- Make a timeline of key events and figures that reflect the history of the counseling discipline. Alternatively, draw a timeline that describes the evolution of a shared professional counseling identity.

- Write an acrostic poem as a group that reflects the goals and objectives of the supervision group's time together.

Activity 2: Gift Giving

Directions: Supervision provides us with what we need to continue to advance in the field of professional counseling. After the past few supervision sessions, your supervisor or a member(s) of your group may have provided you with a gift. These gifts can vary in many ways and often change throughout the supervision time. The gift may be something you needed during a specific session or it may be something you needed throughout your group supervision process. Consider your supervisor and group members. What has the group provided to you? Is there one member in particular that gave you a gift that you really needed? Below are items that you can choose from to give to your colleagues, alternatively you can draw your own item in the space provided.

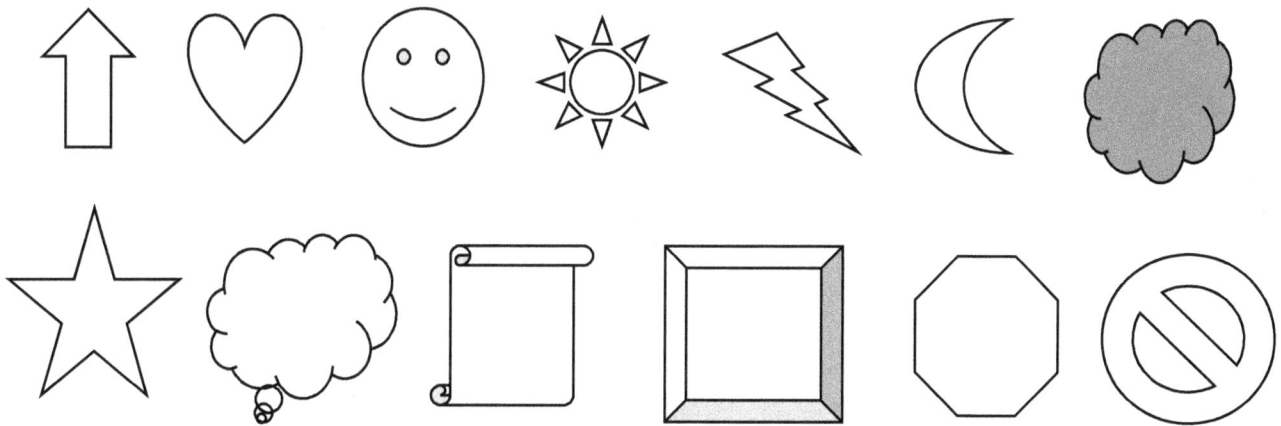

Draw your own gift:

Who will receive your gift?

Processing: Gift Giving

What item did you select as your gift? What does the item represent?

_____

_____

_____

_____

_____

_____

Who did you select to receive your gift? What connected you to that group member?

_____

_____

_____

_____

_____

_____

Have you given any gifts this week?

When you think about the group supervision experience so far, what experience stands out?

_____

_____

_____

_____

_____

_____

As the group supervision experience continues, what gift are you hoping to receive (or continue to receive)?

_____

_____

_____

_____

_____

_____

If you could give multiple gifts, who else might receive one from you? This might be a member of the supervision group or someone else. What would you give to that person, and why?

_____

_____

_____

_____

_____

_____

Taking It to the Group

- What were some of the gifts that were given to the group? What themes emerged as group members first shared their gift selection?

- In what ways has group supervision helped to provide "gifts" to the group members? In what ways does group supervision need to continue to provide "gifts"?

- Allow the group members who received gifts to talk about the impact it has on their own development. What did group members receive? What did getting this gift mean to them? What did it mean to be acknowledged in the group?

- What is advice that the group might offer to new counselors regarding gifts we can provide one another throughout our work?

- How does this notion of "gifting" to one another promote the counseling profession?

My additional thoughts and feelings about the
Gift Giving **activity...**

Supervisor Reflections

Follow-up Supervision Group Activities

- As a group, consider the gifts group members did not receive. Discuss what gifts members may have wanted to receive but did not get.

- This activity can be revisited and conducted again at the end of the semester. Supervisors can bring everyday items into the group experience (i.e., pens, magnets, post it notes, bookmarks, or anything in the office or meeting space). Have students select the item they connect to in the moment and share. After they share, have each member gift their item to someone else in the group.

- Allow group members to select gifts to give themselves. Discuss what they chose and the ways they can work toward getting what they need.

Activity 3: Sharing the View

Directions: Complete the Venn diagram by considering the values and philosophy of professional counseling, as well as your unique identity. List ways that your values and interests, as well as other aspects of your life, overlap with the shared philosophy of professional counseling in the middle space, shared by both circles. Consider factors like your professional interests, strengths, counseling theory, traits, and preferred work setting. Also reflect on the aspects of your life and personality that do not overlap, or that you would prefer to keep separate from your identity as a professional counselor. You might also think about the aspects of professional identity that don't necessarily fit for you (e.g., possible career paths, views).

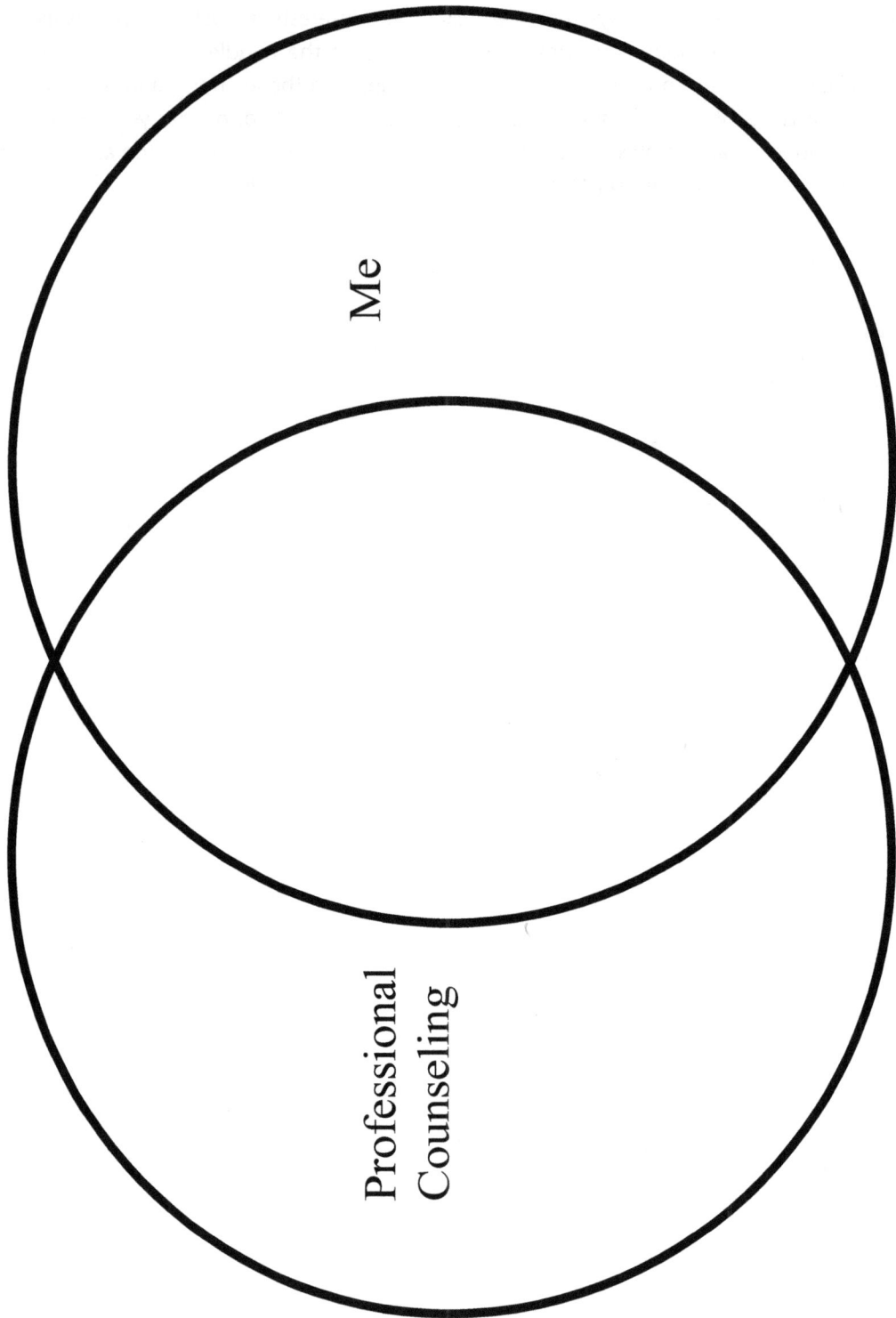

Processing: Sharing the View

In what unique ways do your personal attributes overlap with the shared philosophy of counseling?

_____

_____

_____

_____

List some ways your peers, supervisors, or co-workers see you demonstrating your counselor professional identity.

_____

_____

_____

_____

What did you list in Professional Counseling that did not overlap with your personal attributes and interests? How might this change, or not change, in the future?

_____

_____

_____

_____

Who do you believe has a strong counselor professional identity?

Who is part of the support system that has helped you in your journey to be a professional counselor? Consider personal and professional supports. Who do you hope will continue to support you in the future and what do you need from that person(s)?

Personal:

_____

_____

_____

_____

_____

_____

Professional:

_____

_____

_____

_____

_____

_____

Future:

_____

_____

_____

_____

_____

_____

Taking It to the Group

- What professional identity themes are evident among the group?

- In what ways did group members have similar or different processes in completing the Venn diagram?

- How can group supervision be used to help group members further explore their professional identity development?

- How might considering unique expressions of professional identity inform group members' professional choices (e.g., theories, ACA division involvement, leadership roles, future work places)?

- Why does the group think that counselor professional identity includes the integration of personal attributes, in addition to embracing the shared philosophy and definition of professional counseling?

My additional thoughts and feelings about the
Sharing the View **activity...**

Supervisor Reflections

Follow-up Supervision Group Activities

- Brainstorm a third circle to add to the current Venn diagram. Consider what else might be important to add to this diagram in order to understand professional identity in more complex ways.

- Write an article for your program's newsletter that features the group's discoveries about counselor professional identity and its importance. If your program does not have a newsletter, consider an email blast to share the message.

- Institute *Professional Identity Check-In* time each week the supervision group meets. Take ten minutes for members to report one instance from the previous week, in which their professional identity strengthened.

Activity 4: The Game of Counseling

Directions: Let's play the Game of Counseling! This game will help you explore more pieces about you to continue to develop your professional identity. You will need to answer questions along the way to determine if you move forward or backwards. Make sure to provide the answers to the questions on the board game (see Figure 1.1). Have fun!

Since you began this journey and are willing to move forward, move 2 spaces. ♡ ➡	Is there someone who supports you professionally? Move 3 spaces, if not, move 2 spaces.	If you can identify a supervisor who you connect with, move forward 1 space. If you cannot, move back 1 space.	Identify two areas of expertise that you have. _____ Move forward 2 spaces.	Is there someone who supports you personally? _____ Move forward 1 space.
	Write name here _____	Write Supervisor's name here _____	⬇	Identify one career goal. _____ Move forward 1 space.
What is one area of weakness? _____ Move forward 2 spaces.	If you land here, answer any question you have not yet, then move forward 1 space.	Identify one trigger for you as a counselor. _____ Move forward 2 spaces	What has prevented you from experiencing personal counseling? _____ Move forward one space.	Have you experienced personal counseling before? Yes or No. If yes, move forward 3 spaces. If no, move forward 1 space.
If you land here, answer any question you have not yet, then move forward 1 space. ⬇				
What are two words that connect you to the field of counseling? _____ Move forward 2 spaces	What is your theoretical orientation? _____ If you can't identify it, move backwards 2 spaces. If you can, move forward 1 space.	What is one population that you do not understand? _____ Move forward 1 space	Name one way for you to begin to understand this population. _____ Move forward 2 spaces	Sorry you landed here… move back to any question you did not answer. ⬅
				What is one area of strength for you? _____ Move forward 2 spaces
Congratulations! Your journey to becoming a professional counselor is looking bright! ✴	Did you answer all the questions honestly? If yes, move forward 1 space. If not, move back one space.	Write one reason you did not answer honestly. _____ Move forward 2 spaces.	What is a population you advocate for? _____ Move forward 2 spaces	What is one achievement that you are proud of? _____ Move forward 1 space

Figure 1.1 The Game of Counseling

Processing: The Game of Counseling

Did you make it to the end? Answer any questions that you did not complete.

_____

_____

_____

_____

_____

How do you make connections with others in the field in order to get professional support? How about the connections you make in your life to gain personal support? How do you move forward with your professional goals without support (professionally and personally)?

_____

_____

_____

_____

_____

How did this week feel like a game?

When you think about what you still need to learn about to become a counselor, what immediately comes to mind?

_____

_____

_____

_____

_____

_____

As the group supervision experience continues, what struggles are you willing to share with your group members?

_____

_____

_____

_____

_____

_____

If you could identify two areas to improve upon in your professional identity development, what would those be?

_____

_____

_____

_____

_____

_____

Taking It to the Group

- What were some of the themes shared that described the emerging counselor professional identity from the group?

- In what ways can group supervision provide support to identify group members' triggers? How can the group environment be supportive of sharing these struggles?

- As a group, what career goals are evident? Are there connections among group members? As we consider the personal and professional social supports, how do they support movement towards the goals? Are there any blocks?

- What is some advice that the group might offer to new counselors as they enter the field in creating supportive relationships?

- How is support from others, as well as continued education and awareness pivotal in counselor professional identity development?

My additional thoughts and feelings about
The Game of Counseling **activity...**

Supervisor Reflections

Follow-up Supervision Group Activities

- Share positive achievements with one another. If group members struggle to find achievements, encourage others to offer support in the search, or offer ideas.

- Select the top two themes that the group identified above. Divide the group in half and assign one theme to each group. Allow the group members to debate the themes and identify reasons their theme is most important (e.g., debate the importance and need for supports to professional identity).

- Take time for group members to discuss weak areas, potential triggers, and areas to improve. Discuss ideas to continue to work on these areas, as well as ways to ensure future reflection and examination of areas for continued growth.

References

Auxier, C. R., Hughes, F. R., & Kline, W. B. (2003). Identity development in counselors-in-training. *Counselor Education and Supervision, 43*, 25–38. doi:10.1002/j.1556-6978.2003.tb01827.x

Brott, P., & Myers, J. M. (1999). Development of professional school counselor identity: A grounded theory. *Professional School Counseling, 2*, 339–349.

Burkholder, D. (2012). A model of professional identity expression for mental health counselors. *The Journal of Mental Health Counseling, 34*(4), 295–307. doi:10.17744/mehc.34.4.u204038832qrq131

Burns, S. T. (2017). Crafting a one-minute counselor professional identity statement. *Journal of Counselor Leadership and Advocacy, 4*, 66–76. doi:10.1080/2326716X.2017.1284623

Calley, N. G., & Hawley, L. D. (2008). The professional identity of counselor educators. *The Clinical Supervisor, 27*(1), 3–16. doi:10.1080/07325220802221454

Gibson, D. M., Dollarhide, C. T., & Moss, J. M. (2010). Professional identity development: A grounded theory of transformational tasks of new counselors. *Counselor Education and Supervision, 50*, 2–79. doi:10.1002/j.1556-6978.2010.tb00106.x

Kaplan, D. M., & Gladding, S. T. (2011). A vision for the future of counseling: The 20/20 principles for unifying and strengthening the profession. *Journal of Counseling & Development, 89*, 367–372. doi:10.1002/j.1556-6678.2011.tb00101.x

Kaplan, D. M., Tarvydas, V. M., & Gladding, S. T. (2014). 20/20: A vision for the future of counseling: The new consensus definition of counseling. *Journal of Counseling & Development, 92*, 366–372. doi:10.1002/j.1556-6676.2014.00164.x

Mellin, E. A., Hunt, B., & Nichols, L. M. (2011). Counselor professional identity: Findings and implications for counseling and interprofessional collaboration. *Journal of Counseling & Development, 89*, 140–147. doi:10.1002/j.1556-6678.2011.tb00071.x

Moss, J. M., Gibson, D. M., & Dollarhide, C. T. (2014). Professional identity development: A grounded theory of transformational tasks of counselors. *Journal of Counseling & Development, 92*, 3–12. doi:10.1002/j.1556-6676.2014.00124.x

Nugent, F. A., & Jones, K. D. (2009). *Introduction to the profession of counseling* (5th ed.). Upper Saddle River, NJ: Pearson.

Ponton, R. F., & Duba, J. D. (2009). The ACA code of ethics: Articulating counseling's professional covenant. *Journal of Counseling & Development, 87*, 117–121. doi:10.1002/j.1556-6678.2009.tb00557.x

Prosek, E. A., & Hurt, K. M. (2014). Measuring professional identity development among counselor trainees. *Counselor Education and Supervision, 53*, 284–293. doi:10.1002/j.1556-6978.2014.00063.x

Reiner, S. M., Dobmeier, R. A., & Hernández, T. J. (2013). Perceived impact of professional counselor identity: An exploratory study. *Journal of Counseling & Development, 91*, 174–183. doi:10.1002/j.1556-6676.2013.00084.x

Remley, T. P., & Herlihy, B. (2020). *Ethical, legal, and professional issues in counseling* (6th ed.). Hoboken, NJ: Pearson Education.

Woo, H., & Henfield, M. S. (2015). Professional identity scale in counseling (PISC): Instrument development and validation. *Journal of Counselor Leadership and Advocacy, 2*, 93–112. doi:10.1080/2326716X.2015.1040557

Woo, H., Henfield, M. S., & Choi, N. (2014). Developing a unified professional identity in counseling: A review of the literature. *Journal of Counselor Leadership & Advocacy, 1*, 1–15. doi:10.1080/2326716X.2014.895452

Woo, H., Lu, J., Harris, C., & Cauley, B. (2017). Professional identity development in counseling professionals. *Counseling Outcome Research and Evaluation, 8*(15–30). doi:10.1080/03054985.2017.1297184

Woo, H., Storlie, C., & Baltrinic, E. R. (2016). Perceptions of professional identity development from counselor educators in leadership positions. *Counselor Education and Supervision, 55*, 278–293. doi:10.1002/ceas.12054

CHAPTER 2

SELF-EXPLORATION

Self-exploration is defined as "the examination and analysis of one's own unrealized spiritual or intellectual capacities" (Merriam-Webster, 2019). During the process of self-exploration, people often work to explore all the facets of themselves. This process goes beyond an examination of personality traits, temperament, likes/dislikes, and roles, but also includes considering how culture, beliefs, values, strengths, and experiences culminate to create a person's identity. The process of self-exploration includes self-awareness and self-reflection. The goal of increasing self-exploration is to know one's self better and to bring more of the unknown aspects of self to the forefront of awareness. When people have a clearer vision of their identity, it provides the opportunity to understand themselves better, realize their potential, and identify areas that need more development to be a healthier and more aware person.

Self-exploration is also essential to being an ethical and more aware counselor. Multiple authors support the self-exploration process and value self-examination, specifically when entering the field of professional counseling (Bradley, Whisenhunt, Adamson, & Kress, 2013; Pompeo & Levitt, 2014; Richards, Campenni, & Muse-Burke, 2010; Schmidt & Adkins, 2012). The American Counseling Association Code of Ethics (ACA, 2014) requires counselors to look further at themselves and ensure the work that they conduct imparts no harm to clients. As the process of self-exploration is an ethical obligation within the field, it is promoted and taught accordingly (Schmidt & Adkins, 2012). Counselor education programs accredited by the Council of Accreditation for Counseling and Related Programs are required to teach methods for "personal and professional self-evaluation and implications for practice" (CACREP, 2016, Standard F.1.k). Research has shown that if we do not understand ourselves, we can do harm to our clients, both intentionally and unintentionally (Lawson & Myers, 2011). Therefore, self-exploration can become an important factor in preventing counselor impairment (Bradley et al., 2013) and helping with moral and ethical decision making (Pompeo & Levitt, 2014).

Self-exploration is also important in the development of counselor professional identity, as it can support the achievement of professional growth and goals (Richards et al., 2010). In part, counselor professional identity is an integration of personal and professional selves (Moss, Gibson, & Dollarhide, 2014). The more counselors know about themselves they are able to find their unique connection to, and expression of, their counselor professional identity. The more professional counselors reflect on their personal identities, they will discover how their own experiences, beliefs, values, desires, strengths, and personality fits with that of the profession. This can lead to greater, and more authentic, connections with clients as well as their contributions to, and the roles they take in, the professional counseling field.

Self-exploration can include many components. Continuous reflection on our experiences is one component that is useful for self-examination. Reflection is required for optional learning and exploring personal life experiences and interpersonal sources are influential to our counselor development (Rønnestad & Skovholt, 2003). The process of exploration with counselors can support another person's growth and freedom only to the level that they have maintained their own (Rogers, 1961), emphasizing the need for self-exploration. The process is not only personally rewarding, but also professionally. Personal self-reflection can lead to professional reflection. There is a positive impact on our clients and our own growth and learning (Pompeo & Levitt, 2014). The growth that we experience personally intertwines with our professional work and can lead to greater satisfaction.

Exploring values, beliefs, and biases is also important for counselors as they engage in self-exploration. Mental health professionals support the idea that therapists need to be aware of their own bias and values to be able to appropriately serve their clients (Oden, Miner-Holden, & Balkin, 2009). To do this, we might need to know how we favor certain perspectives or experiences over others. Further, emotional exploration is also important for professional counselors. Holding on to emotions can have lasting effects on the body, not only psychologically, but also physically and mentally. Confronting deepest thoughts and feelings, we can begin to neutralize our mind and body and the associated stressors. Journaling has been helpful for students to expose some of their deeper concerns, struggles, fears, and hesitations that need to be addressed prior to entering the helping profession. The process of identifying emotions protects future clients from counselors who may not be healthy and may, in fact, impart harm via their own negative emotions onto their client (Rust, Raskin, & Hill, 2013).

Exploring labels people use to describe themselves, as well as how others describe them, can also be a component of self-exploration. Labels can influence how individuals understand themselves, how others understand them, and how others relate to them (Malott, 2009). The value that can be placed on these labels can have both a positive and negative impact. As counselors we examine the different sides of ourselves, recognizing these can become barriers to effective counseling (Gray, 2010). Labels are more impactful than many often realize and exploring ones to keep and live up to, as well as those to release, can be an influential factor in personal and professional identity.

For emerging counselors, the field promotes self-exploration and learning to engage in the necessary work of helping others. In order to ensure competence as future counselors, exploring the personal self and identifying unknown areas of influence or parts that require further work is critical in being an ethical and healthy professional counselor, as well as beginning the process of integrating personal and professional identities. The actual process of self-exportation can be difficult. It requires reflection, openness to new awareness, honesty, and critical thinking. Self-exploration can also entail examining influential components of identity, thoughts and emotions, and descriptions and labels imparted by self and others.

Connecting Self-Exploration to You

The actual process of self-exportation can be difficult because there are so many components, but this chapter is dedicated to helping you explore yourself and learn more about who you are. This will help develop your abilities as you progress in your journey to becoming a professional counselor. The intention of this chapter is to help explore your many sides to begin to understand yourself better in your journey to becoming a professional counselor.

Sometimes it is hard to get started on understanding who we are because there are hidden aspects of ourselves. The hidden aspects are the pieces that we want to examine closer because these elements can be impactful on the work we engage in as counselors. When we work with clients, we may find that we experience different emotions that do not always make sense. We may find we feel anxious or angry after a session or have strong feelings towards certain clients. These emotions are often connected to an experience or possibly a belief or value that we hold. Unless we examine ourselves to understand the emotional response we are experiencing, it can make it difficult to know what the response is from. A hazard of this is that we can respond to our client in a negative or harmful way, without meaning to, yet still imparting harm.

Each of the activities in this chapter help you begin to uncover various factors of your personal identity, your beliefs, and what may still be a struggle for you. The activities separate the person and professional counselor to begin unraveling these pieces which we are often not aware exist. The activities might also uncover conflicting pieces of yourself. These pieces may be areas that you want to improve or areas in which you need more knowledge, skill, or awareness because of the negative impact they can have on your clients and professional work.

As a result, the activities in this chapter will help to support your own personal exploration into understanding who you are, what you believe, how you have experienced events, and where you need to move forward. Each activity provides directions, then questions to go further into your responses. The goal is to challenge yourself and be honest so that you are able to grow personally and professionally. You are influenced by those around you, your experiences, your attributes, your values, and your beliefs. You are also influenced by your culture, family/friends, and environment. These pieces all combine to create you. Sometimes, you may see areas that need a little nudge to understand more, a little more knowledge, and a little more work to ensure you can impact your clients in a healthy way (Lawson & Myers, 2011).

Activity 5: Roots to Sky

Directions: Look at the tree on this page. Focus your attention at the bottom of the tree with the roots. Take a second to think about your own roots and who, or what, grounds you. Write these people or things near the roots. Then, moving up the tree to the trunk, think about your core elements. These might be qualities or traits that if you lost, you would lose parts of yourself and what makes you … you. Write these qualities along the trunk. As you continue to move up, consider the branches of your tree. Think about the different identities and interests that are part of you, even if contradictory. Write these things along the branches. Finally, move to the leaves on your tree. Consider some of the areas that you are working on growing, or perhaps some of the areas that you want to lose. Write these among your leaves.

Figure 2.1 Roots to Sky
(Awim, 2019)

Process: Roots to Sky

What similarities or differences do you see in each of the areas of your tree?

Roots:

_____

_____

_____

Trunk:

_____

_____

_____

Branches:

_____

_____

_____

Leaves:

_____

_____

_____

Where have you experienced growth this week?

What area of the tree do you connect to the most? What do you feel most separate from at the moment?

_____

_____

_____

_____

_____

_____

_____

What factors have influenced your leaves, those still growing and those ready to fall off? How do you think these factors will continue to influence your personal self?

_____

_____

_____

_____

_____

_____

_____

_____

When you identified your core, how did it feel to identify what you feel is a true representation of who you are? How do you think this impacts your branches and leaves?

_____

_____

_____

_____

_____

_____

_____

_____

Taking It to the Group

- What themes from the tree (roots, trunk, branches, and leaves) are among the supervision group? How could these themes impact each member's future development as a professional counselor?

- In what ways has group supervision helped identify personal traits or experiences that may need to be further explored?

- Explore the process of growing out some leaves while shedding others. How can group supervision support the process of growing or shedding?

- What is some advice the group might offer through peer supervision in regards to preservation of self, while remaining committed to your counselor professional identity?

- How can the group advocate for clients who are stuck and unable to grow?

My additional thoughts and feelings about the
Roots to Sky activity...

Supervisor Reflections

Follow-up Supervision Group Activities

- Each member of the class can identify one leaf that they want to focus on for the semester. Each member can draw or write out the goal. The instructor can bring these to future meetings. Alternatively, each leaf could be hung in the meeting space.

- At the end of the semester revisit the tree. Allow time for group members to examine what they identified and make any changes. They may want to add, delete, or modify their trees. Spend a few minutes reflecting on their modified trees.

- Create a group tree. What roots the group? What is the trunk/core of the group? What is the group growing towards? What is the group losing?

Activity 6: Put a Pin in It

Directions: As we think of ourselves some labels come to mind. Some of these labels are self-imposed, while others are imposed upon us. Perhaps your label was given to you or maybe it was self-imposed because of experiences or life roles. Some we view as positive and some we may view as negative. Begin to think about the different labels used to describe you, regardless of where they originated. Indicate a label in each note below. Add some additional words, pictures, or anything else that comes to mind when you look at this label.

Processing: Put a Pin in It

What theme do you see among your post it notes? Are there commonalities among how you see yourself versus how others see you?

_____

_____

_____

_____

_____

_____

As you consider each of these labels, do you see any that contradict another?

_____

_____

_____

_____

_____

_____

Where have you experienced these labels this week?

What people, or experiences, have impacted the labels you have given yourself? How so?

_____

_____

_____

_____

_____

_____

Are there any labels you want to change or eliminate? It might be that you want to strip it completely or modify the meaning you have assigned to that label. How could you make the change?

_____

_____

_____

_____

_____

_____

What labels feel true to you and your connection to the field of professional counseling? How do you see this label supporting your professional identity?

_____

_____

_____

_____

_____

_____

Taking It to the Group

- What were some of the labels that members identified? How could these labels impact each members' future development as a professional counselor?

- In what ways has group supervision helped identify labels that may need to be further explored? In what ways do supervisees still need help in understanding the role of these labels on themselves?

- As a group, explore the process of changing some of the labels. How can group supervision support the process of change with the intention of growth?

- What are some ways that peer supervision can uncover any labels, which may contradict our role as a professional counselor?

- What are some labels that professional counseling has been assigned? Are there any that are perceived negatively? If so, how can counselors work to change this perception?

My additional thoughts and feelings about the *Put a Pin in It* activity...

Supervisor Reflections

Follow-up Supervision Group Activities

- Each member of the class can identify one label they have assigned to another group member. Spend time discussing the label and the impact it has on the group member.

- At the end of the semester revisit the notes. Have each member indicate where they have seen a change in their labels and how they were able to accomplish this change.

- As a group, create labels for the field and highlight one to work towards embodying (if it is a positive label) or changing (if it is a negative label) throughout the semester.

Activity 7: My Emerging Self

Directions: Self-awareness and growth is important for counselor professional identity. For this activity consider your personality, natural abilities, and interests. Also think about your changes since beginning your counselor education program. Using any creative medium (e.g., writing, art, collage), represent yourself in the below categories and on the back of this page.

My natural talents and qualities are:	
My personality traits are:	

My interests are:	What I have learned about myself throughout graduate school is:	I chose a career in counseling because:

Processing: My Emerging Self

What answers in this activity do you like, and what things do you want to change?

_____

_____

_____

_____

_____

_____

What personal attributes do you believe are going to help and inform you as a counselor?

_____

_____

_____

_____

_____

_____

How have you experienced the importance of self-awareness or change this week?

In what ways have some of your personality traits, natural qualities, and interests influenced your choice to become a counselor?

_____

_____

_____

_____

_____

_____

How have you learned about these qualities, value, interests, and other things about yourself?

_____

_____

_____

_____

_____

_____

_____

In completing this activity, what new aspects did you learn about yourself?

_____

_____

_____

_____

_____

_____

Taking It to the Group

- What were some commonalities found among the group answers for the last column of the activity?

- How did individuals in the group become aware of their personal attributes, values, and motivations?

- During group supervision, how can a self-reflective environment be cultivated? What makes a self-reflective setting so important to the supervision process?

- What can be done to ensure group members continue to be self-aware and engaged in self-reflection? How can they encourage other counselors in their future work settings to do the same?

- How does the group define the importance of self-exploration during the process of becoming a counselor?

**My additional thoughts and feelings about the
My Emerging Self activity...**

Supervisor Reflections

Follow-up Supervision Group Activities

- In pairs, complete interviews to learn about each other's personal qualities and interests. Provide feedback on how these attributes contribute to, and shine through, the interviewee's counseling style.

- Research the qualities and traits of professional counselors and determine how these traits are evidenced in individuals in the supervision groups.

- Create personal time capsules at the beginning and end of the supervision course to track how supervisees change and re-describe themselves over time.

Activity 8: Personal Philosophies

Directions: Counselor professional identity consists of embracing the definition and philosophy of professional counseling, as well as integrating personal beliefs and attributes with that of the profession. Consider what you have learned about yourself in this chapter, as well as what you learned about professional counseling in the previous chapter to complete the speech bubbles below.

1. I decided to be a counselor because…

2. Professional counseling differs from other helping professions in the following ways…

3. I'm a good occupational fit for professional counseling because …

4. Effective professional counselors are able to…

5. The qualities I possess that will help me to develop into an effective counselor are…

6. My master's program has influenced my ideas about professional counseling in the following ways…

Processing: Personal Philosophies

Which speech bubble was the easiest for you to answer, and which was the hardest?

Number _____ was the easiest because

_____

_____

_____

_____

Number _____ was the hardest because

_____

_____

_____

_____

What connections are there between answers about you (numbers 1, 3, 5) compared to answers about the professional counseling discipline (numbers 2, 4, and 6)?

_____

_____

_____

_____

In what ways have you demonstrated your beliefs about counseling this week?

How has your answer to number 6 evolved from the beginning of your professional counseling master's program to now?

_____

_____

_____

_____

What are influencing factors from your personal, professional, and academic life that helped you form your answers?

Personal:

_____

_____

_____

_____

Professional:

_____

_____

_____

_____

Academic:

_____

_____

_____

_____

Taking It to the Group

- What are themes found among group members' activities or processing questions?

- What commonalities or differences exist in the how group members described the influence of their coursework, internship, and academic experiences on how they view themselves and their fit with the profession?

- Among the group, which questions were hardest and easiest to answer? What does the group attribute to the ease and difficulty of these particular questions?

- Consider some advice for incoming students. How would the group advise beginning professional counseling students to make the most of their master's program in order to learn about themselves and how they fit with the field?

- How is counselor self-awareness and growth related to counseling professional identity?

**My additional thoughts and feelings about the
Personal Philosophies activity...**

Supervisor Reflections

Follow-up Supervision Group Activities

- When is self-reflection more difficult? What factors make it easier? Discuss ways to encourage reflection among the group, as well as how to facilitate it with others.

- Together, write an advertisement for your professional counseling program that highlights the professional and personal growth gained throughout the program in graduating with a master's degree.

- Create a group-authored thank you note for individuals the group identifies as influential in personal and professional growth.

References

American Counseling Association. (2014). *Code of ethics*. Retrieved from: www.counseling.org/resources/aca-code-of-ethics.pdf

Awim. (2019). Tree vector silhouette with black and white [JPEG]. Retrieved from www.shutterstock.com/image-vector/tree-vector-silhouette-black-white-1380779969

Bradley, N., Whisenhunt, J., Adamson, N., & Kress, V. E. (2013). Creative approaches for promoting counselor self-care. *Journal of Creativity in Mental Health, 8*(4), 456–469. doi:10.1080/15401383.2013.844656

Council for Accreditation of Counseling and Related Educational Programs. (2015). *2016 CACREP Standards*. Retrieved from http://www.cacrep.org/wp-content/uploads/2018/05/2016-Standards-with-Glossary-5.3.2018.pdf

Gray, R. (2010). Shame, labeling and stigma: Challenges to counseling clients in alcohol and other drug settings. *Contemporary Drug Problems, 37*(4), 685–703. doi:10.1177/009145091003700409

Lawson, G., & Myers, J. E. (2011). Wellness, professional quality of life, and career-sustaining behaviors: What keeps us well? *Journal of Counseling & Development, 89*(2), 163–171. doi:10.1002/j.1556-6678.2011.tb00074.x

Malott, K. M. (2009). Investigation of ethnic self-labeling in the Latina population: Implications for counselors and counselor educators. *Journal of Counseling & Development, 87*(2), 179–185. doi:10.1002/j.1556-6678.2009.tb00565.x

Merriam-Webster. (2019). Self-exploration. Retrieved from www.merriam-webster.com/dictionary/self-exploration

Moss, J. M., Gibson, D. M., & Dollarhide, C. T. (2014). Professional identity development: A grounded theory of transformational tasks of counselors. *Journal of Counseling & Development, 92*, 3–12. doi:10.1002/j.1556-6676.2014.00124.x

Oden, K. A., Miner-Holden, J., & Balkin, R. S. (2009). Required counseling for mental health professional trainees: Its perceived effect on self-awareness and other potential benefits. *Journal of Mental Health, 18*, 441–448. doi:10.3109/09638230902968217

Pompeo, A. M., & Levitt, D. H. (2014). A path of counselor self-awareness. *Counseling and Values, 59*(1), 80–94. doi:10.1002/j.2161-007x.2014.00043.x

Richards, K., Campenni, C. E., & Muse-Burke, J. (2010). Self-care and well-bring in mental health professionals: The mediating effects of self-awareness and mindfulness. *Journal of Mental Health Counseling, 32*(3), 247–264. doi:10.17744/mehc.32.3.On31v88304423806

Rogers, C. (1961). *On becoming a person*. New York, NY: Houghton Mifflin.

Rønnestad, M. H., & Skovholt, T. M. (2003). The journey of the counselor and therapist: Research findings and perspectives on professional development. *Journal of Career Development, 30*, 5–44. doi:10.1023/A:1025173508081

Rust, J. P., Raskin, J. D., & Hill, M. S. (2013). Problems of professional competence among counselor trainees: Programmatic issues and guidelines. *Counselor Education and Supervision, 52*(1), 30–42. doi:10.1002/j.1556-6978.2013.0026.x

Schmidt, C. D., & Adkins, C. P. (2012). Understanding, valuing, and teaching reflection in counselor education: A phenomenological inquiry. *Reflective Practice: International & Multidisciplinary Perspectives, 13*, 77–96. doi:10.1080/14623943.2011.626024

CHAPTER 3

COUNSELOR WELLNESS

Wellness is related to overall well-being and health in mind, sprit, and body. There are many factors to obtaining and maintaining wellness, and it is often referred to as a holistic and multi-faceted concept. Myers, Sweeney, and Witmer (2000) described wellness as

> a way of life oriented toward optimal health and well-being in which mind, body, and spirit are integrated by the individual to live more fully within the human and natural community. Ideally, it is the optimum state of health and well-being that each individual is capable of achieving.

(p. 252)

For counselors, wellness is a key aspect of our professional identity, and its focus is integral in distinguishing the counseling discipline from other helping professions (Mellin, Hunt, & Nichols, 2011). Professional counselors promote wellness with their clients from a preventative standpoint in order to enhance self-care and well-being (Remley & Herlihy, 2020). Incorporating wellness into client conceptualizations, treatment planning, and counseling sessions is not only imperative in the work counselors do with clients, but a distinguishing aspect of counselor professional identity.

Research has suggested that wellness is not only an important factor to promote with clients, but also a necessity for counselors. Self-care and the quest for wellness is an area in which counselors must *walk the talk*. The American Counseling Association Code of Ethics (2014) underscores wellness as a professional responsibility by indicating counselors must practice self-care in order to be aware of, and sustain, their well-being. The Council for Accreditation of Counseling and Related Programs standards (2016) also includes the importance of counselor trainees learning strategies for self-care. These ethical and educational recommendations are supported as impaired counselors can harm clients (Lawson, Venart, Hazler, & Kottler, 2007), but well counselors can more easily promote client wellness (Hill, 2004; Witmer & Young, 1996). Further, higher levels of counselor wellness lead to positive counseling outcomes such as stronger therapeutic alliance (Roach & Young, 2007) and overall counselor competency (Lawson, 2007).

Despite its advantages, professional counselors might sometimes find it difficult to sustain wellness. New counselors often report high burnout (Craig & Sprang, 2010), as do counselors who hold large caseloads and work with high-risk clients (Lawson & Myers, 2011). The day-to-day stress of a counseling job can also lead to more impairment (Lambie, 2007). Though counselors promote wellness for clients, due to the susceptibility to impairment and burnout, professional counselors may sometimes minimize the importance of their own self-care and struggle with maintaining wellness (Lawson et al., 2007; Meyer & Ponton, 2006).

Researchers have attempted to identify specific techniques and behaviors counselors use in order to create and maintain wellness. Through an empirical investigation into counselor wellness, Lawson (2007) found that spending time with family/partners, having a sense of humor, being self-aware, maintaining a sense of control over work, and balancing professional and personal lives were factors that led to participants' wellness. Lawson and Myers (2011) also examined counselor behaviors that led to wellness. Their findings corroborated those reported by Lawson (2007), though they added to the mounting list of wellness related activities by indicating that participants who engaged in quiet leisure activities, reflected on present experiences, remained objective with clients, and held strong professional identity also reported stronger wellness and self-care.

In their study of factors leading to minority female counselor educators' wellness, Shillingford, Trice-Black, and Butler (2013) learned that participants aimed to protect their boundaries, connect with factors that motivated them to excel, keep a positive support system, develop self-care plans, and hold strong professional identities. Additional literature has indicated other strategies for counselor wellness including celebrating accomplishments and being attuned to mind, body, and emotion (Venart, Vassos, & Pitcher-Heft, 2007) and improving working conditions and practices in mindfulness (Thompson, Amatea, & Thompson, 2014).

All of the aforementioned factors leading to wellness are exciting and hopeful. Though, professional counselors may struggle with wellness due to the high demands of the job, there are many factors that can be integrated into daily life that can promote wellness and self-care. What is striking about the list of wellness related activities in the previous paragraphs are that they are versatile and all-encompassing. There are activities related to mindset and perspective (e.g., celebrating accomplishments, remaining objective with clients), relationships and connectedness with others (e.g., support systems, spending time with loved ones), intrapersonal factors (e.g., reflection, being attuned to emotion, self-awareness, mindfulness), and professional activities (e.g., control over work, improving work conditions, professional identity). This might be useful as professional counselors find unique aspects of wellness that fits well for them, while perhaps being inspired by research in the area of counselor wellness.

The versatility in wellness factors also provides evidence that wellness is holistic and should be infused in many factors of one's life and being. Theory-based and empirically supported, The Indivisible Self Model of Wellness (IS-WEL; Myers & Sweeney, 2004) provides construct and structure to understanding and promoting wellness in multiple areas of one's life. This model describes wellness as a holistic phenomenon, in which many components of self are seen as integrative in order to create overall wellness for a person. This model has 5 factors (e.g., social, essential, coping, physical, and creative), each with related supporting domains. Each factor and associated domain is viewed in context of self, community, and society and is interdependent on the other factors in order to enhance wellness (Myers & Sweeney, 2004).

Blount and Lambie (2018) also suggested that holistic wellness is related to different factors through their Helping Professional Wellness Discrepancy Scale (HPWDS). This scale measures helping professionals' perceived and aspiration wellness in an effort to make more informed decisions and actions toward wellness. The HPWDS measures wellness through the following domains: (a) professional and personal development activities, (b) religion/spirituality, (c) leisure activities, (d) burnout, and (e) optimism (Blount & Lambie, 2018, p. 14).

Both of the above models demonstrate the importance of infusing wellness into many aspects of one's life and not only relying on one or two areas (e.g., just using exercise or time with friends) for overall wellness. These are just a couple of various models of wellness that are available and researched. When considering wellness models, though, Day-Vines and Holcomb-McCoy (2007) warned that most do not account for racism, as well as multicultural definitions of wellness; therefore, learning about unique aspects of wellness for individuals amidst societal and cultural impacts is imperative. For example, Jang, Lee, Puig, and Lee (2012) determined that Korean counselors demonstrated differences in wellness than their American counterparts and suggested that differences in wellness exist among collectivist and individualistic cultural groups. This demonstrates the importance of taking culture into account when promoting wellness and for counselors to find their unique and individual ways to incorporate it into their lives in ways that fit best.

Wellness is an important aspect of counselor professional identity, as it is included in the fundamental definition and philosophy of the profession. Professional counselors aim to promote wellness in their clients, though in order to do so, they must remain cognizant of their own wellness and self-care. Research has been helpful in the area of counselor wellness, as it offers models to conceptualize and assess wellness, as well as offer specific tactics for counselors to remain well amidst the demands of the profession. Interestingly, research provides evidence that counselors who hold a strong professional identity tend to report higher levels of wellness (Lawson & Myers, 2011; Shillingford et al., 2013). This further promotes the usefulness of developing professional identity as a counselor and reiterates the importance of wellness.

Connecting Wellness to You

Throughout this chapter you will be encouraged to explore wellness and self-care and learn tactics that might be useful as you continue in your career. Activities were created to help you become more aware of wellness and learn more about your unique styles of self-care. Each are grounded in the recommendations summarized above for obtaining and maintaining wellness. For example, you will be asked to consider your unique emotional needs and desires when it comes to wellness so that you can eventually find self-care tactics that uniquely fit you. Another activity focuses on concrete goals to change your mindset and perspective when coping with stress, which can be a useful skill when stress in the workplace arises. Being able to connect to accomplishments and professional belonging is important for professional identity development, as well as avoiding burnout. As such, you will be asked to track your accomplishments and feelings of contribution or "fit" with your counseling work throughout one week. As challenges often hold our attention more than accomplishments, this list can help you see all of the wonderful work you are doing and all the contributions you are making even when things seem difficult. Finally, you will be asked to consider your unique needs of wellness in various domains to promote wellness in multiple facets of your life. The goal of the culmination of the activities is to help you consider wellness as an important part of your professional identity and way of being as a professional counselor.

Activity 9: Color My Heart

Directions: Think back to when you were accepted into graduate school to begin your quest to become a professional counselor. What were your motivations to be a professional counselor? What feelings come to mind as you think about that moment and time in your journey? In the first heart, write/draw all the feelings you experienced at that time. Also indicate your motivation in embarking on this journey. Then, think about this moment right now. You are getting closer to your goal of becoming a professional counselor. What are you feeling at this moment in your journey? In the second heart, write/draw all the feelings you are currently experiencing. Feel free to use colors, pictures, or anything to illustrate your hearts.

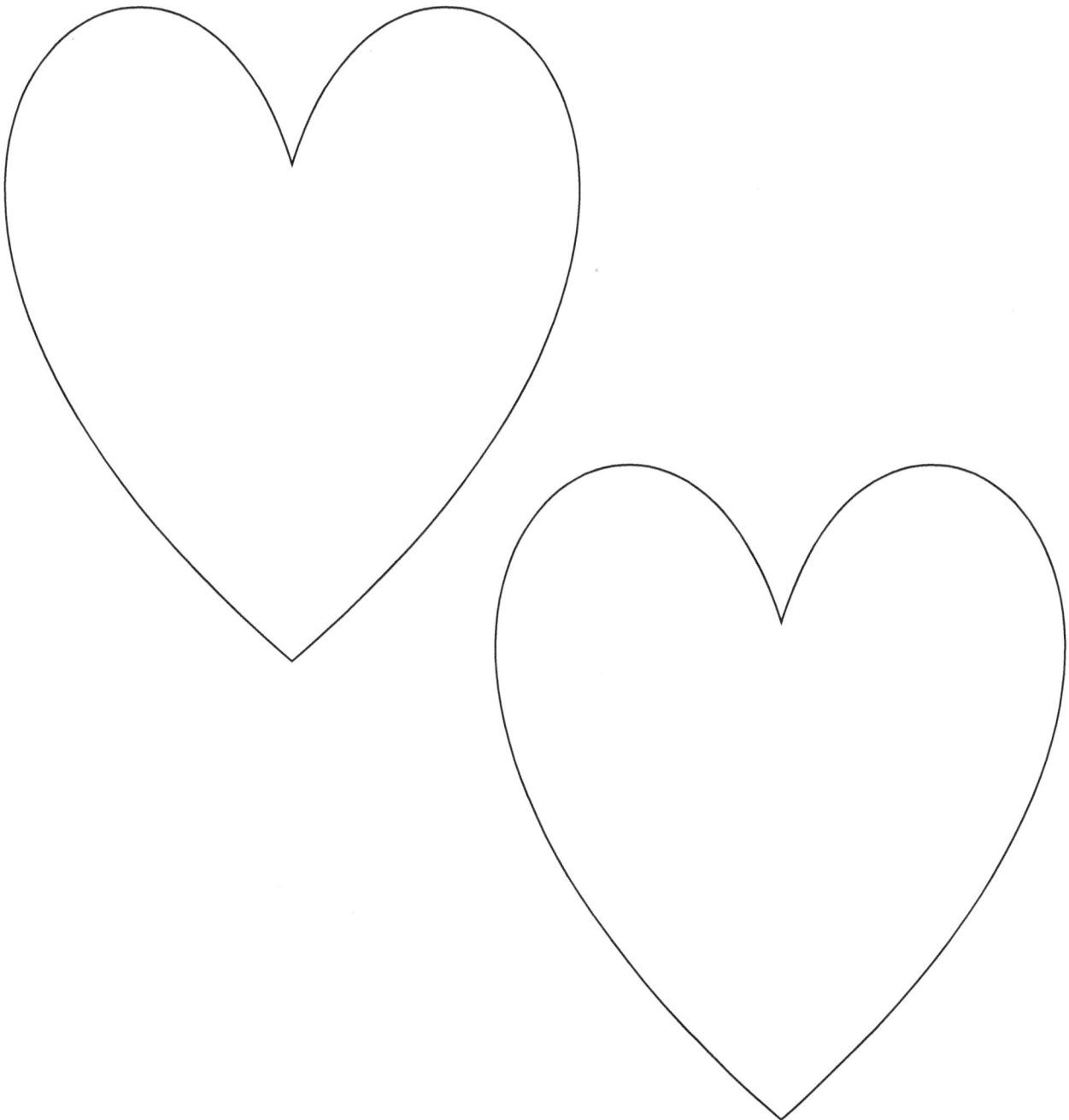

Processing: Color My Heart

Compare and contrast your two hearts. What is the same? What is different?

_____

_____

_____

_____

_____

When you started on this journey, what were your motivations to enter the field? How have these stayed the same, strengthened, or changed?

_____

_____

_____

_____

_____

_____

What has your heart experienced this week?

How does it feel to reconnect to your motivations in becoming a professional counselor? When are times when you might lose track of these motivations and need to be reminded?

_____

_____

_____

_____

_____

_____

When you reflect on your current heart, what emotional challenges do you see?

_____

_____

_____

_____

_____

_____

As you are closer to the end of your journey to become a professional counselor, where do you still need to grow in your heart? What areas do you need to continue working on?

_____

_____

_____

_____

_____

_____

Taking It to the Group

- What were some of the early feelings and emotions that the group identified as they began their journey to become a professional counselor? What were some common motivating factors that led group members to pursue a career in professional counseling?

- How does the group think that connecting to the motivations, or factors, that led you to be a counselor is helpful for wellness? What are some self-care strategies that the group engages in, in order to stay connected to members' motivations in becoming a counselor?

- As a group, explore the experiences that have changed some of the feelings from the first heart to the current heart. Who or what factors have contributed to changed feelings? Are group members still motivated to become professional counselors?

- What is some advice that members can seek from peers or supervisors regarding the emotions this journey in becoming a professional counselor has evoked?

- What are some ways the group can advocate for clients to engage in self-care activities?

My additional thoughts and feelings about the
Color My Heart **activity...**

Supervisor Reflections

Follow-up Supervision Group Activities

- Have group members identify their favorite song that helps them to relax and stay connected to their goals. Select a few songs to play during the group and share the feelings evoked.

- It is important for group members to process their feelings regarding the impact their journey has had on their development in a safe, appropriate place. Spend time talking about the importance of continued supervision and/or personal counseling in a quest for wellness.

- Wellness practices are useful to counselors. Engage in meditation as a group for a few minutes. Turn off lights, noises, and distractions. Allow the group to sit in silence for 5 minutes to center their breathing and connect to themselves.

Activity 10: Framing It Out

Directions: Stress is part of everyone's life and not all stress is negative. Learning to manage your stress is essential to self-care and emotional health. Sometimes it's useful to reframe our stress in order to begin to tackle it. In the space provided below, note areas of stress or struggle you have. Then, spend time thinking about how you can reframe the stress into something useful or perhaps eliminate it.

List the stresses and struggles that stop you from moving forward.

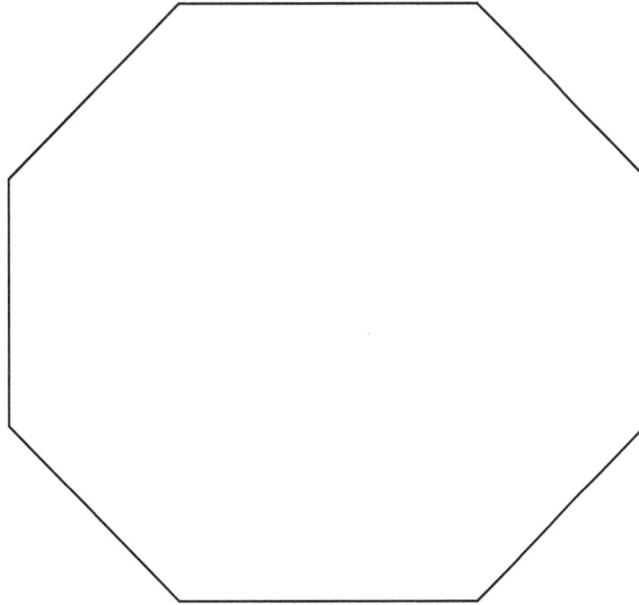

Reframe the stresses and struggles.

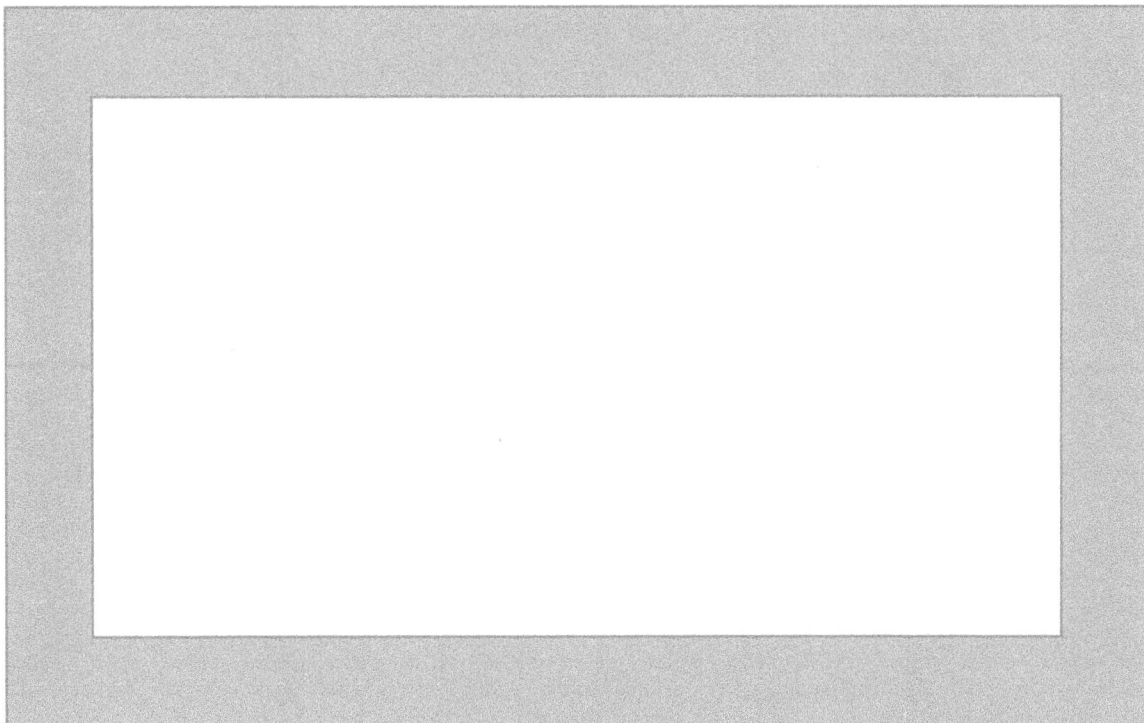

Processing: Framing It Out

How did it feel to write out your current areas of stress or struggle?

_____

_____

_____

_____

_____

_____

When you read what you wrote regarding your stress, does it feel possible that you can reframe it?

_____

_____

_____

_____

_____

_____

Where, when, or how have you experienced stress this week?

Describe the process you went through to reframe your stress and/or struggles.

_____

_____

_____

_____

_____

_____

What was difficult when you reframed your stress/struggles?

_____

_____

_____

_____

_____

_____

_____

In looking at the new view of your stress/struggles, what feelings are you experiencing?

_____

_____

_____

_____

_____

_____

Taking It to the Group

- What were some of the themes that emerged for group members in regard to their stresses and/or struggles?

- Discuss the emotions that were evoked as group members began to identify what they are currently experiencing. What impact did these emotions have on the group members?

- As a group, explore the process of reframing the stress and/or struggles into something more manageable or potentially eliminating it completely. Are there areas where group members were unable to find a way to reframe the stress? If so, spend time helping that group member reframe the stress/struggle.

- What is some advice that the group might offer to an incoming practicum or internship group regarding stress and how to manage it at this phase in your professional identity development journey?

- How can the group advocate for more support from employers to recognize the importance of stress management for employees?

My additional thoughts and feelings about the
***Framing It Out* activity...**

Supervisor Reflections

Follow-up Supervision Group Activities

- If anyone is struggling to identify areas of stress/struggle, allow group members to help identify stress. Alternatively, continue to work on ways to reframe the areas that members are stuck, especially as it may impact their own wellness.

- Using imagery, such as a balloon floating away or the sun rising, may help bring a sense of calm to the group after a discussion that is sometimes emotionally charged. Give this a try any time the group is experiencing stress or talking about a difficult topic.

- Allow each group member to have 30 seconds at the start of each group meeting to decompress and share anything before beginning group supervision. This will provide an opportunity to let go of anything they have brought, focusing on the present.

Activity 11: Identifying Success and Finding Your Place

Directions: Acknowledging positive experiences and finding belonging in your job are contributing factors to wellness. On the strips of space outlined below, list the successes and contributions you have had over the week. Upon completion, consider cutting the strips out and placing them in an envelope or flag this page in the book. You can look back on this collection of positive experiences to reconnect with your successes when you are feeling unmotivated or discouraged in your work.

A positive experience at my internship or counseling job this week was:	
A positive experience at my internship or counseling job this week was:	
A positive experience at my internship or counseling job this week was:	
A positive experience at my internship or counseling job this week was:	
I contributed to my counseling site or profession this week by:	
I contributed to my counseling site or profession this week by:	
I contributed to my counseling site or profession this week by:	
I contributed to my counseling site or profession this week by:	

Processing: Identifying Success and Finding Your Place

After looking back at the accomplishments and success you listed, what do you find surprising? What did you expect?

_____

_____

_____

_____

What feelings and thoughts do you have after looking over the week's list?

Feelings:

_____

_____

_____

_____

Thoughts:

_____

_____

_____

_____

How did you acknowledge your success, as well as those of others, this week?

Who at your site may have noticed these things without you knowing? What do you think this person (or these people) saw in you to recognize these accomplishments?

_____

_____

_____

_____

_____

_____

How does examining the contribution you made toward your site helpful in finding a sense of belonging at site, or even in the field of counseling?

_____

_____

_____

_____

_____

_____

How will you know when to look back at this list? When might you need some reminders of your accomplishments and sense of belonging in the field or at your work site?

_____

_____

_____

_____

_____

_____

Taking It to the Group

- How does the group believe connecting with a sense of belonging can lead to wellness?

- In what ways is strength-based supervision, in which strengths and successes are highlighted, useful for counselor wellness?

- How can the group cultivate a strength-based and accomplishment focused supervision experience? How might this be useful for the group's time together?

- What advice does the group have for a counselor struggling to identify their strengths, successes, and sense of belonging in the field or workplace?

- What are ways that counseling professional identity, or the shared definition and philosophy of counseling, include wellness as an overall theme?

My additional thoughts and feelings about the
Identifying Success and Finding Your Place **activity...**

Supervisor Reflections

Follow-up Supervision Group Activities

- Commit to cultivating a strength-based group experience. What can individual group members do to create this environment? What is necessary to maintain this ethos throughout the group's time together?

- Consider celebrating a "Counselor of the Week." The identified counselor can highlight successes of the week, describe ways he or she overcame obstacles, and share other important accomplishments.

- Make a collective positive experiences box for the group. Have each group member write a success from the week on a slip of paper and place it in the box. At the end of each month members can take turns reading entries.

Activity 12: Self-Care That Fits for You

Directions: Consider wellness and self-care activities that fit and suit you well. You might find inspiration in research about tactics that professional counselors use in order to maintain wellness, or you might consider the things you are already doing to demonstrate self-care. After considering some of your unique strategies for wellness and self-care, create a wellness plan in the spaces provided below and on the back. As wellness is a holistic endeavor that reaches multiple aspects of one's life, you are asked to come up with five ways to engage in wellness across different self-identified domains in your life (e.g., relationships, intrapersonal, work, body/physical, thoughts). If you need help coming up with five different areas, look up holistic models of wellness to give you some ideas.

Wellness Area 1:

Goal:

What is one objective for achieving this goal?

What is something you already do to work toward this goal?

Wellness Area 2:

Goal:

What is one objective for achieving this goal?

What is something you already do to work toward this goal?

Wellness Area 3:

Goal:

What is one objective for achieving this goal?

What is something you already do to work toward this goal?

Wellness Area 4:

Goal:

What is one objective for achieving this goal?

What is something you already do to work toward this goal?

Wellness Area 5:

Goal:

What is one objective for achieving this goal?

What is something you already do to work toward this goal?

Processing: Self-Care That Fits for You

How did you determine your five separate areas for self-care? Keeping in mind that wellness is holistic, how will these five separate areas contribute to your overall well-being?

_____

_____

_____

_____

_____

How is your plan unique and individualized for you? How do your unique attributes, identity, and culture provide the foundation for your plan?

_____

_____

_____

_____

_____

When have you implemented your self-care plan this week?

You were asked to consider ways that you were already working on self-care in your identified areas. How was this helpful for you in your process of creating your wellness plan?

_____

_____

_____

_____

_____

_____

What obstacles do you anticipate in your wellness and what will you do to overcome them?

_____

_____

_____

_____

_____

_____

Who will help you achieve your goals? How will you know when you need to reach out or seek some support?

_____

_____

_____

_____

_____

_____

Taking It to the Group

- What did the group learn about the holistic nature of wellness in competing this activity?

- How did group members ensure that their self-care plans were customized to their unique identities and needs?

- What needs to continue, or what needs to change, in group supervision to maintain professional counselor wellness as a priority?

- How can counselor wellness cultivate client wellness? What factors are important to ensure that this message of wellness and its importance is modeled and associated with the counseling profession?

- In what ways is wellness uniquely associated with counselor professional identity?

My additional thoughts and feelings about the
Self-Care That Fits for You activity...

Supervisor Reflections

Follow-up Supervision Group Activities

- How can group members help each other sustain their self-care plans? Spend time checking-in with each other to follow up on the plans and offer support if needed.

- Make a group commitment to wellness by completing one wellness activity, or related conversation, during each class meeting. Consider rotating activities and topics to meet various domains of wellness.

- Create a wellness day for the group, counseling program, or community. Highlight multiple aspects of wellness and spread the message of self-care to other counselors.

References

American Counseling Association (2014). 2014 *Code of ethics*. Retrieved from www.counseling.org/resources/aca-code-of-ethics.pdf

Blount, A. J., & Lambie, G. W. (2018). Development and factor structure of the helping professional wellness discrepancy scale. *Measurement and Evaluation in Counseling and Development, 51*, 92–110. doi:10.1080/07481756.2017.1358060

Council for Accreditation of Counseling and Related Educational Programs. (2016). *CACREP accreditation standards and procedures manual*. Alexandria, VA: Author.

Craig, C. D., & Sprang, G. (2010). Compassion satisfaction, compassion fatigue, and burnout in a national sample of trauma treatment therapists. *Anxiety, Stress & Coping, 23*, 319–339. doi:10.1080/10615800903085818

Day-Vines, N. L., & Holcomb-McCoy, C. (2007). Wellness among African American counselors. *Journal of Humanistic Counseling, Education and Development, 46*(1), 82–97. doi:10.1002/j.2161-1939.2007.tb00027.x

Hill, N. R. (2004). The challenges experienced by pretenured faculty members in counselor education: A wellness perspective. *Counselor Education and Supervision, 44*, 135–146. doi:10.1002/j.1556-6978.2004.tb01866.x

Jang, Y. J., Lee, J., Puig, A., & Lee, S. M. (2012). Factorial invariance and latent mean differences for the five factor wellness inventory with Korean and American counselors. *Measurement and Evaluation in Counseling and Development, 45*(2), 71–83. doi:10.1177/0748175611427915

Lambie, G. W. (2007). The contribution of ego development level to burnout in school counselors: Implications for professional school counseling. *Journal of Counseling & Development, 85*, 82–88. doi:10.1002/j.1556-6678.2007.tb00447.x

Lawson, G. (2007). Counselor wellness and impairment: A national survey. *Journal of Humanistic Counseling, Education and Development, 46*, 20–34. doi:10.1002/j.2161-1939.2007.tb00023.x

Lawson, G., & Myers, J. E. (2011). Wellness, professional quality of life, and career-sustaining behaviors: What keeps us well? *Journal of Counseling & Development, 89*, 163–171. doi:10.1002/j.1556-6678.2011.tb00074.x

Lawson, G., Venart, E., Hazler, R. J., & Kottler, J. A. (2007). Toward a culture of counselor wellness. *The Journal of Humanistic Counseling, Education and Development, 46*, 5–19. doi:10.1002/j.2161-1939.2007.tb00022.x

Mellin, E. A., Hunt, B., & Nichols, L. M. (2011). Counselor professional identity: Findings and implications for counseling and interprofessional collaboration. *Journal of Counseling & Development, 89*, 140–147. doi:10.1002/j.1556-6678.2011.tb00071.x

Meyer, D., & Ponton, R. (2006). The healthy tree: A metaphorical perspective of counselor well-being. *Journal of Mental Health Counseling, 28*, 189–201. doi:10.17744/mehc.28.3.0341ly2tyq9mwk7b

Myers, J. E., & Sweeney, T. J. (2004). The Indivisible Self: An evidence-based model of wellness. *Journal of Individual Psychology, 60*(3), 234–245.

Myers, J. E., Sweeney, T. J., & Witmer, J. M. (2000). The wheel of wellness counseling for wellness: A holistic model for treatment planning. *Journal of Counseling & Development, 78*, 251–266. doi:10.1002/j.1556-6676.2000.tb01906.x

Remley, T. P., & Herlihy, B. (2020). *Ethical, legal, and professional issues in counseling* (6th ed.). Hoboken, NJ: Pearson Education.

Roach, L. F., & Young, M. E. (2007). Do counselor education programs promote wellness in their students? *Counselor Education and Supervision, 47*, 29–45. doi:10.1002/j.1556-6978.2007.tb00036.x

Shillingford, M. A., Trice-Black, S., & Butler, S. K. (2013). Wellness of minority counselor educators. *Counselor Education and Supervision, 52*, 255–269. doi:10.1002/j.1556-6978.2013.00041.x

Thompson, I. A., Amatea, E. S., & Thompson, E. S. (2014). Personal and contextual predictors of mental health counselors' compassion fatigues, and burnout. *Journal of Mental Health Counseling, 36*(1), 58–77. doi:10.17744/mehc.36.1.p61m73373m4617r3

Venart, E., Vassos, S., & Pitcher-Heft, H. (2007). What individual counselors can do to sustain wellness. *Journal of Humanistic Counseling, Education and Development, 46*, 50–65. doi:10.1002/j.2161-1939.2007.tb00025.x

Witmer, J. M., & Young, M. E. (1996). Preventing counselor impairment: A wellness approach. *Journal of Humanistic Education and Development, 34*, 141–155. doi:10.1002/j.2164-4683.1996.tb00338.x

CHAPTER 4

ETHICS AND COUNSELING

Ethics is an important area in the field of professional counseling. CACREP (2016) requires academic programs to meet specific learning objectives related to ethics (Section.2.F.1). In almost all academic classes, there are discussions regarding ethics and their impact on clients. As the ACA (2014) Code of Ethics notes, "professional values are an important way of living out an ethical commitment" (p. 3). Ethics help frame decision-making, create relationships with our clients, and provide counseling services to best meet client needs. The ACA Code of Ethics (American Counseling Association, 2014) supports the work of professional counselors, framing the basis of our work with clients, and providing clarity in times of confusion (Ametrano, 2014).

Effective counselors possess sound ethical and legal knowledge and because of this they have the ability to integrate their work with diverse clients in various settings (Lambie, Hagedorn, & Ieva, 2010). Most ethical violations or misconduct are issues with professional identity and the effects of inadequate training of the counselor (Even & Robinson, 2013). As counselors continue to develop their self-knowledge, they take extra steps to ensure that they are not imposing their values on clients and providing best care (Francis & Dugger, 2014). New counselors entering the field work towards reconciling their personal values and culture-of-origin beliefs to follow the standards set forth by the counseling profession (Ametrano, 2014).

Counselors rely on their professional identity as a frame of reference as they engage in ethical decision making, with awareness to their limitations and personal experiences (Moss, Gibson, & Dollarhide, 2014). Emerging counselors have been found to make ethical decisions using a combination of personal values, the client's best interests, transparency in decision making, and perceptions of formal training and practice (Levitt, Farry, & Mazzarella, 2015). This combination demonstrates an intentional reflection in making ethical decisions, recognizing the personal self of the counselor and providing a balance of the client's needs and obligation within the field. Many emerging counselors reported a disconnect between training and reality when faced with ethical decisions and were able to use transparent methods to support their client (i.e., consultation with supervisors or colleagues, review of the ACA Code of Ethics, referrals to other professionals, and open communication with the client). While personal values entered into the process of ethical decision making, it appeared to be more in deducing next steps and understanding the experience presented by the client (Levitt et al., 2015).

To be ethical, professional counselors often withhold their own values, judgments, and personal opinions in their counseling relationships. The counseling process is about clients and their own journey, without the impact of their counselor. Importantly the therapeutic relationship is an essential component of the counseling process, and research would argue the most important part of the counseling relationship (Sommers-Flanagan, 2015). A clear piece of this relationship is non-judgment from the counselor and removal of the counselor's own values. This is an area where intentionality is required to address the impact of personal values or beliefs intersecting with ethical requirements in the counseling profession (Ametrano, 2014).

The process of self-exploration is an ethical obligation within the field (Schmidt & Adkins, 2012). Integrating personal self-exploration with the ethical standards helps to examine oneself through a different lens. It also helps one to understand how to process difficult client cases, bridging together training and reality (Heller et al., 2015). Research has shown academic programs spend time emphasizing different cases and teaching how to apply ethical standards to make appropriate decisions, yet, emerging counselors still feel disconnected and at times unprepared when faced with the ethical situations. Some of these discrepancies may have a connection to personal views imposed upon clients, not necessarily that they are unclear of the ethical obligations or the ACA Code of Ethics (2014). Regardless of this, spending time exploring personal experiences will provide more counselor clarity and separation from client (Drew, Stauffer, & Barkley, 2017).

As professional counselors, we are obligated to each of the standards listed in the ACA Code of Ethics (2014) and there are consequences to not adhering to them. Some of the consequences may be more personal, taking care of yourself because unhealthy counselors produce unhealthy clients (Lawson & Myers, 2011). Other ethical violations can result in ethics hearings from state boards and suspended or revoked licenses. As professional counselors we are obligated to provide the highest quality of care to our clients at all times (Gutierrez & Mullen, 2016) and ensuring we are not imparting harm. Therefore, by exploring the relationship between oneself and the ethical code, it begins to provide clarification by applying each standard to ourselves.

Connecting Ethics to You

The activities in this chapter are aimed at helping you examine how ethical obligations frame our work as professional counselors. Oftentimes the ethical standards seem removed from the work we do and may present themselves in very specific situations (i.e., client in danger, boundary issues, or breach of confidentiality). The potential pitfalls of ethical violations, however, can emerge in ways we did not imagine. Sometimes, too, personal experiences or areas we haven't explored within ourselves can leave us vulnerable to ethical challenges. When these times present themselves, we may not be ready to address them or, more commonly, we are not even aware that they exist.

The reflections and activities in this chapter challenge you to consider any experiences or feelings you may have that can lead to ethical pitfalls and then reexamine them through the frame of ethical boundaries. Simple questions of, "How do I respond when a client is experiencing the same issue that I have?" "How do I support my client when I feel that they need to do the opposite of what they are doing?" or "How do I work with my client when they are triggering a painful experience for me?" might be all it takes to help bring these situations into your awareness. These questions often feel removed as you are embarking on your new journey toward becoming a professional counselor, yet they may emerge for each of you at different times. The intention is to understand how your unique experiences may impact your ethical relationship with clients. Beginning to work towards recognizing, resolving, and reworking those experiences so that you are prepared and competent to follow ethical obligations is important.

Considering ways to avoid ethical dilemmas and be prepared for them is also an important skill for counselors. In the chapter you will be asked to anticipate some ethical challenges and brainstorm possible solutions by using a variety of resources. Further, you'll be prompted to create an ethics alter ego to move you into "action mode" when you sense an ethical challenge emerging. Ultimately, by the end of this chapter you will not only further explore the ACA (2014) Code of Ethics as professional responsibility and part of your counselor professional identity, but also increase your awareness to potential ethical challenges and prepare for dilemmas in the future.

Activity 13: Ethics Cartoons

Directions: Consider the ACA (2014) Code of Ethics and identify at least three areas to learn more about or you believe will be relevant to you. Create cartoon scenarios in the space provided on the back of this page depicting how you might find yourself in related ethical dilemmas. Using resources, provide a potential solution to each dilemma in the fourth box. Remember to title your cartoons and ensure they have a beginning, middle, and end.

Title

Title

Title

Processing: Ethics Cartoons

What themes are evident in your cartoons? This might include emotions, content, characters, or tone of the cartoon.

_____

_____

_____

_____

_____

_____

How do these themes reflect some of your worries, excitement, or concerns about your counseling work?

_____

_____

_____

_____

_____

_____

_____

Where and when did you observe a counselor using ethical practice this week?

Review the 2014 ACA Code of Ethics and list the relevant ethical codes for each cartoon.

_____

_____

_____

_____

_____

_____

List at least three sources you have to help solve each ethical dilemma.

_____

_____

_____

_____

_____

_____

As ethical dilemmas often have many potential ways to be solved, choose one cartoon and write an alternate ending.

_____

_____

_____

_____

_____

_____

Taking It to the Group

- What are some common themes in the ethical dilemmas created by group members? How might these themes reflect the counselor developmental level of each group member?

- Throughout this activity, what did group members learn about seeking ethical support?

- How did group members collectively experience the importance of ethics throughout the week?

- In what ways can the American Counseling Association provide ethical support to counselors? What other ethics resources did group members identify?

- How is ethical practice critical in the professional identity of counselors?

My additional thoughts and feelings about the *Ethics Cartoons* activity...

Supervisor Reflections

Follow-up Supervision Group Activities

- For this ethics activity you had to come up with an alternate ending to one of your cartoons. Discuss the gray areas of ethics and ways to navigate various possibilities when it comes to solving ethical dilemmas.

- Investigate the ACA ethics hotline. Consider ethical dilemmas that might be brought to the hotline and role-play the parts of ethics officers and counselors.

- As a group, consider having a "Dear Abby" inspired ethics column in your program or site's newsletter. Others can write in ethical questions that group members can answer or fictional ethical dilemmas can be presented. If no newsletter exists, brainstorm an alternative outlet to serve this purpose (e.g., a weekly email, posting on a bulletin board).

Activity 14: Symbolism

Directions: There are important components in the process of creating professional selves and identities. Some aspects are the ones you have learned throughout your academic journey, like counseling skills and concepts. Other aspects come from self-reflection and understanding yourself and how it connects to the counseling profession. We have many dimensions to our personal and professional selves, which impact the professional work we do. Looking at these areas can open your eyes to areas of ethical vulnerability.

For this next activity, answer each question on the back of this page. You may draw a picture or symbol to represent your answer or you can write a word or two. Don't spend too much time thinking about your responses, rather, write down the first words/symbols that come to mind for each prompt.

Something you would like to change about you

Populations of people you feel strongly about

"Me" the visible counselor

"Me" the hidden counselor

Client emotion that may affect your professional work

Professional Strengths

A challenge you have communicating with clients

Something about your work that inspires you

A behavior you have that makes your professional role difficult

A concern you have about your career journey

Processing: Symbolism

What was it like to respond to each question with limited time for reflection?

_____

_____

_____

_____

_____

_____

As you look at your symbols, what themes emerge?

_____

_____

_____

_____

_____

_____

What symbol did you see this week?

What prompts were more challenging? Discuss that struggle you experienced in answering those prompts.

_____

_____

_____

_____

_____

_____

If you have to select one area to further reflect on, which one would you choose and why?

_____

_____

_____

_____

_____

_____

Reflecting on your answers, what area(s) might be more vulnerable to ethical violations and cause you to seek supervision more readily? What are some possible ethical dilemmas that might arise or situations in which you may need to be more cautious?

_____

_____

_____

_____

_____

_____

Taking It to the Group

- Have each group member share their response to each question. Spend time discussing and drawing parallels between students.

- What prompt was most difficult? What made this one more difficult than others (the prompt or the answer)? Spend time talking through the challenging areas.

- As a group, explore the questions regarding change further. What would change look like in your professional world and what are the steps?

- What is some advice that group members can offer one another regarding potential areas of ethical vulnerability and safe guards to ethical practices?

- How does the group believe self-awareness can lead to being a more ethical counselor? How does this, in turn, help to advocate for clients and the counseling profession?

**My additional thoughts and feelings about the
Symbolism activity...**

Supervisor Reflections

Follow-up Supervision Group Activities

- As a group, spend time discussing the client emotion that may affect professional work. What are safeguards that can protect us and create appropriate boundaries to avoid potential ethical violations?

- Look at the ACA Code of Ethics (2014). Have group members match their symbols to areas in the code where potential violations may occur.

- Create a list of strategies to address potential ethical violations identified in the above activity.

Activity 15: Superhero Alter Ego

Directions: Ethical dilemmas can motivate a counselor to go into *"action mode."* The counselor must consider the situation, gather information, use ethical decision-making models, and turn to support in order to make a clear and concise plan. Create your own ethics superhero alter ego, to turn into when ethical *"action mode"* is necessary. In the space provided below draw your superhero emblem. Think of a motto for your superhero and write it in the banner below. You can also name your superhero.

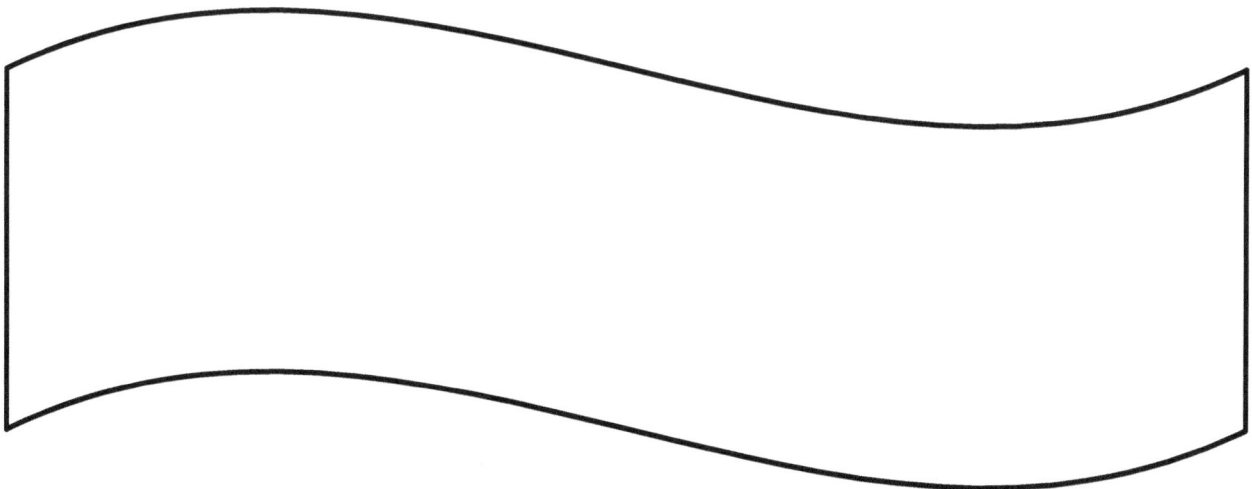

Processing: Superhero Alter Ego

How is your superhero's motto reflective of your desires to be an ethical counselor?

_____

_____

_____

_____

_____

_____

Which of your strengths shine through your superhero alter ego?

_____

_____

_____

_____

_____

_____

When did your superhero emerge this week?

How will you know when to turn into your superhero?

_____

_____

_____

_____

_____

_____

How will others know that your superhero is coming to solve the ethical dilemma? What will they see you doing?

_____

_____

_____

_____

_____

_____

What is the "kryptonite," or threat, to your superhero, and how will you ward against it?

_____

_____

_____

_____

_____

_____

Taking It to the Group

- As a group, what strengths were identified as integral to the success of members' superheroes?

- What were some common signs group members identified to indicate that an ethical dilemma might be impending? What are some ideas to be on guard for these signs, as to avoid an ethics situation?

- What can group members do to promote ethics awareness and support for other new counselors or at everyone's counseling sites?

- What advice would the group give to other counselors regarding threats to ethical behavior?

- How does ethical problem solving promote counseling professional identity and counseling philosophical tenets?

My additional thoughts and feelings about the
Superhero Alter Ego **activity...**

Supervisor Reflections

Follow-up Supervision Group Activities

- Examine your state licensing board website for common ethics violations. Learn the ethics investigation process and potential consequences in your state. Discuss ways to avoid ethical pitfalls.

- Create a name for your band of superheroes and create a shared vision and mission statement. Discuss how to use this vision and mission when you are each acting individually as professional counselors.

- Make up ethical case studies to present to a panel of your superheroes. While group members are acting as their superheroes, they can respond to the ethical dilemmas in unique ways.

Activity 16: Center of You

Directions: Reflect on a personal experience that has been impactful to you and your identity (i.e., adoption, divorce, abuse, addiction, mental health, loss, etc.). Note this experience in the center circle. You will not be asked to share this experience, unless you choose. Then, move about the circle to reflect the *positive* impact this experience had on you, as well as your future role as a professional counselor. There is also space to consider how this experience can be related to being an ethical counselor.

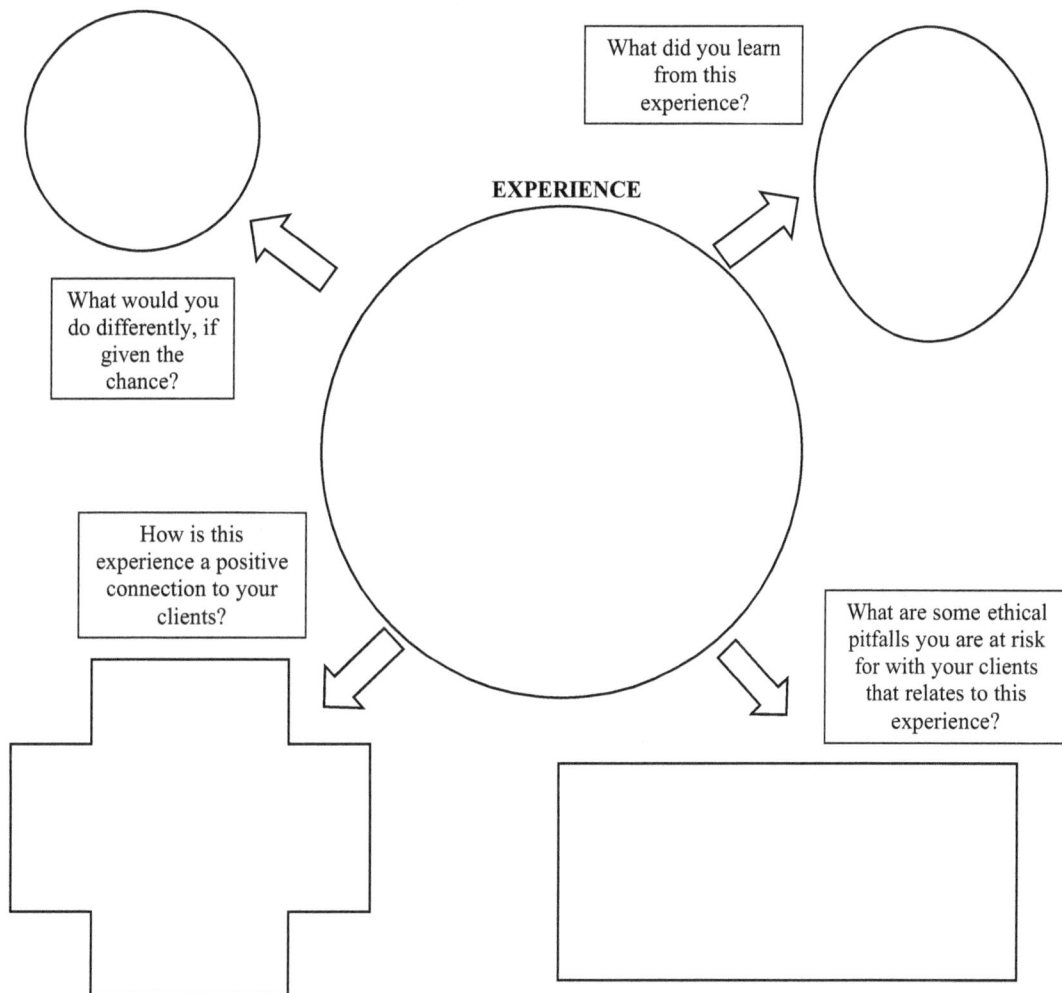

What did you learn from this experience?

EXPERIENCE

What would you do differently, if given the chance?

How is this experience a positive connection to your clients?

What are some ethical pitfalls you are at risk for with your clients that relates to this experience?

Processing: Center of You

What was it like to identify and write about your experience?

_____

_____

_____

_____

_____

_____

In this activity, you wrote about something you learned from the identified experience. Is there an area in your life where you believe this "lesson" has been the most impactful? If so, what is it?

_____

_____

_____

_____

_____

_____

What is one positive thing you did this week that can be connected to this experience?

Which question in this activity was challenging to answer? What meaning do you give this challenge?

_____

_____

_____

_____

_____

Sometimes impactful experiences are out of our control. How can you work with clients who have experiences that are out of their own control in an effort to help them make meaning from it?

_____

_____

_____

_____

_____

Step back and reflect on the potential ethical pitfalls that you could experience as counselor that is related to this experience (e.g., boundaries) and list relevant ethical codes. What could you do to prevent these from occurring?

_____

_____

_____

_____

_____

Taking It to the Group

- Have group members volunteer to share their experience (do not force sharing if group members are not willing). Work with each other to make connections between experiences and ensuring ethical counseling.

- What has been a defining moment for the group's time together? What did the group learn from this experience and how does it continue to impact the group?

- Defining moments or experiences can shape our future and our beliefs. Sometimes we are unaware of its influence or impact on future experiences, and in some instances, it might unknowingly have a negative impact. Discuss the value of personal counseling on efforts to be an ethical counselor and the development of counselor professional identity.

- What is some advice that the group might offer to new counselors emerging in the field regarding personal experiences and upholding ethical codes as outlined by ACA (2014)?

- Looking at the history of counseling, what are some defining moments for the profession that impacted its future?

My additional thoughts and feelings about the *Center of You* activity...

Supervisor Reflections

Follow-up Supervision Group Activities

- Allow the group the opportunity to reflect on their identified experiences. Does anyone want to change the impact the experience had? If so, what would they do differently if given the opportunity (e.g., actions, reactions, etc.)? Connect this to their future work with clients.

- As a group, create a resource list for counselors. This should include counselors, advocacy centers, and emergency services.

- Work as a group to identify ethical interventions to use with clients. This can reframe their own experience into a productive strategy for clients.

References

American Counseling Association. (2014). *Code of ethics*. Retrieved from www.counseling.org/resources/aca-code-of-ethics.pdf

Ametrano, I. M. (2014). Teaching ethical decision making: Helping students reconcile personal and professional values. *Journal of Counseling & Development, 92*(2), 154–161. doi:10.1002/j.1556-6676.2014.00143.x

Council for Accreditation of Counseling and Related Educational Programs. (2016). *CACREP accreditation standards and procedures manual*. Alexandria, VA: Author.

Drew, M., Stauffer, M. D., & Barkley, W. (2017). Personal counseling in academic programs with counselor trainees. *The Journal of Counselor Preparation and Supervision, 9*(1). doi:10.7729/91.1131

Even, T. A., & Robinson, C. R. (2013). The impact of CACREP accreditation: A multiway frequency analysis of ethics violations and sanctions. *Journal of Counseling & Development, 91*, 26–34. doi:10.1002/j.1556-6676.2013.00067.x

Francis, P. C., & Dugger, S. M. (2014). Professionalism, ethics, and value-based conflicts in counseling: An introduction to the special section. *Journal of Counseling & Development, 92*, 131–134. doi:10.1002/j.1556-6676.2014.00138.x

Gutierrez, D., & Mullen, P. R. (2016). Emotional intelligence and the counselor: Examining the relationship of trait emotional intelligence to counselor burnout. *Journal of Mental Health Counseling, 38*(3), 187–200. doi:10.1774/mehc.38.3.01

Heller, D. L., Farry, T. J., & Mazzarella, J. R. (2015). Counselor ethical reasoning: Decision-making practice versus theory. *Counseling and Values, 60*(1), 84–99. doi:10.1002/j.2161.007x.2015.00062.x

Lambie, G. W., Hagedorn, W. B., & Ieva, K. P. (2010). Social-cognitive development, ethical and legal knowledge, and the ethical decision making of counselor education students. *Counselor Education and Supervision, 49*(4), 228–246. doi:10.1002/j.1556-6978.2010.tb00100.x

Lawson, G., & Myers, J. E. (2011). Wellness, professional quality of life, and career-sustaining behaviors: What keeps us well? *Journal of Counseling & Development, 89*, 163–171. doi:10.1002/j.1556-6678.2011.tb00074.x

Levitt, D. H., Farry, T. J., & Mazzarella, J. R. (2015). Counselor ethical reasoning: Decision-making practice versus theory. *Counseling and Values, 60*(1), 84–99. doi:10.1002/j.2161-007x.2015.00062.x

Moss, J. M., Gibson, D. M., & Dollarhide, C. T. (2014). Professional identity development: A grounded theory of transformational tasks of counselors. *Journal of Counseling & Development, 92*, 3–12. doi:10.1002/j.1556-6676.2014.00124.x

Schmidt, C. D., & Adkins, C. (2012). Understanding, valuing, and teaching reflection in counselor education: A phenomenological inquiry. *Reflective Practice: International and Multidisciplinary Perspectives, 13*(1), 77–96. doi:10.1080/14623943.2011.626024

Sommers-Flanagan, J. (2015). Evidence-based relationship practice: Enhancing counselor competence. *Journal of Mental Health Counseling, 37*(2), 95–108. doi:10.17744/mehc.37.2.g13472044600588r

CHAPTER 5

MULTICULTURAL AWARENESS

Multiculturalism has multiple definitions evolving over time in the counseling profession. There are different definitions depending on the application of multiculturalism, but simplistically it reflects distinct cultural and ethnic groups within a society. For the counseling profession, multiculturalism has grown to include not only multiple identities (i.e., racial, ethnic, gender, sexual, socioeconomic, age, religions, disabilities), but also the intersection of these identities to privileged and marginalized statuses (Ratts, Singh, Nassar-McMillan, Butler, & McCullough, 2016) and multicultural awareness. Multicultural awareness is the impact that personal experiences and values can have on the counseling relationship (Atkins, Fitzpatrick, Poolokasingham, Lebeau, & Spanierman, 2017). This broad definition (multiculturalism and multicultural awareness) acknowledges the wide-angle lens approach that is required to fully develop multicultural competence as an emerging counselor.

As the United States continues to change in demographics, pressures on counselors to continue to develop their multicultural competence to meet the needs of changing clients persist (Ahmed, Wilson, Henriksen, & Jones, 2011). Failure to address personal bias and prejudices or the inability to engage in difficult dialogues related to race and culture may result in a negative therapeutic alliance (Sue, Torino, Capodilupo, Rivera, & Lin, 2009). The inability to promote clients damages professional identity, ethical obligations (ACA, 2014), and standards identified by CACREP (2016, Section 2.F.2). Strategies for effective multicultural and social justice counseling suggest acknowledging personal fears and challenges to work through the bias. In the area of multicultural and social justice awareness, emerging counselors may often assume that they do not carry bias and dismiss the reflection needed in this area. Counselors who follow a color-blind strategy towards different racial groups actually impart detrimental effects into the counseling relationship instead of examining their own beliefs and experiences (Atkins et al., 2017). Examining how you identify within your world and the connection to the counseling profession to examine your hidden self (Chan, Cor, & Band, 2018) is essential in the development of counselor professional identity. Multicultural counseling competence can be difficult, but ensures a commitment to the ACA Code of Ethics (2014) in examining how counselors' personal selves and the harm they may impart by imposing beliefs or experiences onto our clients. Research has found that counselors who work collaboratively with clients to understand their worldview, regardless of expertise or experience, yield more successful outcomes (Hook, Davis, Owen, Worthington, & Utsey, 2013).

The journey towards multicultural and social justice counseling competence is long and requires personal changes, along with professional changes, to address hidden bias and work towards a resolution (Shannonhouse & West-Olatunji, 2013). Self-refection is a basic competency of all counselors, regardless of experience in the field (Ahmed et al., 2011). There are various strategies and tools that can support the discovery, and heightened awareness, of self and areas of bias held by professional counselors and counselor trainees. One of these effective tools is writing, which has been found to help change these assumptions counselors may hold and process related experiences. Shannonhouse, Barden, and Mobley (2015) used specific journaling prompts to process a multifaceted, multicultural immersion experience with the intention to "evaluate strengths and needs as professional counselors and to deepen the understanding of ethical and clinical implications of working with diverse populations" (p. 306). Techniques like journaling provide an opportunity for counselors to process their responses to multicultural experiences and acknowledge areas of weakness.

Emerging counselors struggle with the concepts of understanding their own privilege and commitment to social justice as they enter the field. Often emerging counselors might feel resistant towards acknowledging their own experiences of privilege, but examination is necessary towards developing competence (Estrada, Poulsen, Cannon, & Wiggins, 2013). Multicultural and social justice competence is regarded as a lifelong process to continuously work on understanding and practicing cultural humility (Ratts et al., 2016). As counselors learn about their own assumptions, experiences, values, and cultural beliefs, they begin to accept their own actions and inactions that are inherent within and the impact on clients (Matthews, Barden, & Sherrell, 2018; Shannonhouse & West-Olatunji, 2013). Multicultural awareness also expands to include examining experiences of privilege, with the intention to move counselors towards being social justice advocates (Chan et al., 2018). As the research suggests, understanding yourself is necessary to move towards achieving multicultural awareness and ultimately competence. This is inclusive of social justice and our own areas of privilege and oppression (Ratts & Greenleaf, 2018). As counselors, we acknowledge the areas of privilege in our lives and recognize the impact that it has on our own work. These open and hidden experiences impact the work we do with our clients (Shannonhouse & West-Olatunji, 2013).

Advocacy is a core component to professional identify as counselors. Lewis, Ratts, Paladino, and Toporek (2011) defined advocacy as "a natural outgrowth of the counselor's empathy and experience" (p. 9). This definition combined with the ACA's Advocacy Competencies (2018) provides a framework for incorporating advocacy into a counselor's work. The ACA Advocacy Competencies (2018) have two primary functions. First, advocacy is for, or on the behalf of, a client or community. Second, advocacy is an intervention. The intervention can be on the individual, systemic, or societal level. As counselors, it is essential to recognize that any advocacy effort is informed by the client and not based on a counselor's determination. Importantly, advocacy requires skills that are the result of training, knowledge, understanding of human behavior, communication skills, systems competence, and a connection to organizations (Lewis et al., 2011). As counselors, we are in a position to advocate for our clients because these are critical components to our training.

The Multicultural and Social Justice Counseling Competencies (MSJCC) recognize that counselors "must evolve to address the needs of culturally diverse clients and social justice concerns that both shape and contextualize mental health and overall well-being" (Ratts et al., 2016, p. 30). Additionally, the counseling profession follows the competencies for transgender clients (ALGBTIC, 2010) and competencies for counseling with lesbian, gay, bisexual, queer, questioning, intersex, and ally individuals (Harper et al., 2013). There are also spiritual and religious counseling competencies (Cashwell & Watts, 2010). Counselors are committed to working with all clients, understanding the unique needs of clients, and advocating for clients. It is important to acknowledge the multiple oppressions that marginalized individuals experience and advocating for counseling settings for all clients.

In our commitment to becoming competent counseling professionals, we commit to understanding ourselves. The process of self-reflection is critical in our development and necessary to ensure the focus remains on clients. We recognize the emotional connection we have in our life and our experiences. This recognition should also move to work on examining areas that need further attention to ensure we are healthy individuals. This work ensures we are providing the highest quality of care to our clients (Gutierrez & Mullen, 2016).

Connecting Multicultural Awareness to You

Each of the activities within this chapter examines the ethical components of counseling and the impact to your own professional identity. The underlying assumption, in which they are based, is that we need to learn and explore different cultures to understand experiences other than our own. While it is essential to understand the client and their identity, it is equally important to ensure you examine your beliefs and the impact it has on your work as a professional counselor. In our work, who we are and the way we respond directly impacts our clients. This includes our theoretical orientation and how we view clients, it also includes how our life experiences impacts us and what the experience has taught us. The lessons gained from those experiences may not be positive and have left unresolved issues that need to be examined. As these unresolved issues emerge, you have the opportunity to repair the holes and become whole and make meaning of the experiences.

The activities have the intention to push you to look deeper at your beliefs, experiences, thoughts, and perceptions to examine areas that need to be examined closer. Identifying early memories and experiences to determine what areas you need support in (by way of education or personal reflection) will aid you to become a multiculturally aware and competent counselor. Connecting with your own culture is also important as you become aware of all the aspects of yourself that you bring to the counseling relationship. Further, taking a closer look at some of the biases or fears you have can also challenge your perceptions. Being uncomfortable can lead to growth, so be sure to be honest and take chances. All of this can translate into supporting clients in their journey and keeping your journey out of their process.

Activity 17: The Hidden Self

Directions: As individuals, we are multifaceted. We have pieces of ourselves that we make visible to everyone. These are the pieces that we feel the most comfortable with others seeing. Alternatively, there are pieces of ourselves we keep hidden. These are the pieces we do not want to share with others. Our resistance to sharing these pieces can be because we fear we will not be accepted, we are embarrassed/shameful, or we do not think it is important to reveal. For this activity there is a mask below, as well as one on the backside of this page. For the first mask below, identify five pieces of you that you show the world. These can be attributes, roles, labels, or other part of your identity that is visible to others. For the second mask on the back, identify five pieces you hide from the world. These can be attributes, roles, labels, or other parts of your identity that are not visible to the world. You will not be required to share your hidden self with the group.

Figure 5.1 Visible Mask
(Daksun, 2019)

Figure 5.2 Hidden Mask
(Daksun, 2019)

Processing: The Hidden Self

What is one piece of your visible mask that you want the world to see the most?

_____

_____

_____

_____

_____

_____

What is one piece of the hidden mask that you are most protective of and work to ensure it is not visible?

_____

_____

_____

_____

_____

_____

_____

How did you uncover your mask this week?

What do you feel when you examine your hidden mask?

_____

_____

_____

_____

_____

_____

How do you think the pieces of your hidden self could negatively impact the work you do with your clients?

_____

_____

_____

_____

_____

_____

Can you imagine sharing your hidden self? What do you think would happen if you made these pieces visible?

_____

_____

_____

_____

_____

_____

Taking It to the Group

- As a group, share your visible masks. Do you see any themes emerging, specifically as future professional counselors? What feels safe about the visible self?

- Reflecting on the hidden self (no group member is required to share any details of their hidden self), what emotions emerge when revealing it to others?

- As a group, spend time processing possible outcomes for revealing some aspects of the hidden self. This does not require sharing specific pieces, but more of an overall response to the feared outcomes of revealing the hidden self.

- What is some advice that the group might offer to an incoming practicum or internship group regarding the relationship between your visible and hidden self and its impact on clients?

- What are some ways the group can advocate for additional multicultural educational workshops? In what ways is continued education about multiculturalism important to counselor professional identity?

My additional thoughts and feelings about
The Hidden Self activity...

Supervisor Reflections

Follow-up Supervision Group Activities

- As group members share some of the emotions evoked at the possibility of revealing the hidden self, connect this to the experience that clients feel in revealing their full self to a counselor. How can we support clients sharing fully in counseling if we feel blocked?

- Identify three interventions that can be used with clients to help uncover their hidden self.

- Have group members share a piece of the visible self they see in one another. This can provide each group member with additional insight on how others see their selves.

Activity 18: My Cultural Self

Directions: Consider your cultural identity. Think of a representation of this identity and put a picture and/or description of it below. You might choose a specific cultural item that represents this part of you. Alternatively, you can use a symbol, song, picture, poem, game, or cultural story.

Processing: My Cultural Self

Cultural identity is intersectional and made up of many aspects. What parts of your identity are not captured in your representation of this activity?

_____

_____

_____

_____

_____

_____

What were some critical events when you became aware of either your cultural identity or the awareness of racial and cultural differences in your life? This could also include aspects of privilege and oppression.

_____

_____

_____

_____

_____

_____

When have you felt connected to your cultural identity this week?

How has awareness of your own, and others', cultural experiences changed or been confirmed throughout your counselor education studies?

_____

_____

_____

_____

_____

_____

Is there a part of your cultural identity that you may want to shed? What would the impact of shedding this part of your cultural identity be in your life?

_____

_____

_____

_____

_____

_____

Are there ways that your cultural identity may have an impact on your counseling work? Consider both positive and negative ways.

_____

_____

_____

_____

_____

_____

Taking It to the Group

- Take turns discussing your cultural identity representations and share things that you learned about each other.

- What were some common experiences group members had in identifying and processing their cultural symbols and cultural identity development?

- How can the group improve discussion of culture and its influence on professional identity during group supervision?

- What can group members do to advocate and promote cultural, racial, and social awareness in counseling?

- In what ways does counseling professional identity include multicultural and social awareness?

**My additional thoughts and feelings about the
My Cultural Self activity...**

Supervisor Reflections

Follow-up Supervision Group Activities

- How does counselors' awareness of their cultural identities positively impact their ability to counsel and connect with clients? Discuss ways to improve connection with cultural identity in order to be a multicultural and social justice counselor.

- Spend a group meeting dedicated to cultural identity. Group members can choose to share representations of their identity with the group through song, dance, education, food, or any other means available.

- Plan and execute a multicultural or social advocacy program or mission to meet the unique needs of your local community. This may include connecting with your town mayor to learn about current needs of the community or maybe a cultural immersion activity or outing.

Activity 19: The Body

Directions: The body below represents you. Within the body, write or draw your personal attributes, values, and cultural beliefs. Once the inside is completed, on the outside of the body, write or draw the attributes, values, and cultural beliefs that are different or opposite to your own.

Figure 5.3 The Body
(Hliv, 2019)

Processing: The Body

As you compare your inner body to the outer body, what cultural conflicts appear?

_____

_____

_____

_____

_____

_____

How can you begin to address the discrepancies that exist between yourself and your potential clients?

_____

_____

_____

_____

_____

_____

_____

Where have you experienced a clash of beliefs this week?

In what ways might the discrepancies you noted in the last question impact your work?

_____

_____

_____

_____

_____

_____

How will you address these areas to ensure you are meeting the needs of your clients?

_____

_____

_____

_____

_____

_____

Do you see any other areas of potential bias or conflict that you need to address? If so, how can you begin to address these areas?

_____

_____

_____

_____

_____

_____

Taking It to the Group

- We all have experiences that impact our beliefs. Often, we are afraid to acknowledge the areas of potential bias. Spend time discussing these areas.

- What areas of difference between your body and the outside space stood out to you? What areas of similarity were there?

- Is there an area where you feel you would not be able to work with a client fitting this description?

- What is some advice that the group might offer to an incoming practicum or internship group regarding the relationship between their beliefs and those of their clients?

- What is the group's stance on requiring professional counselors to be in counseling to assist counselors in addressing their biases?

My additional thoughts and feelings about
The Body activity...

Supervisor Reflections

Follow-up Supervision Group Activities

- As group members share, challenge them to reflect on past experiences that may initiate a response that could become a potential area for bias and impact their work with clients.

- Hold an article review club. Have group members research an area of values bias or cultural bias and share it with the group.

- Allow each group member the space to share attributes, beliefs, or values they struggle to support and competently counsel. As a group, discuss ways to support each member's ability to move past bias, or preference to our own ideas, to further develop counseling competence.

Activity 20: Sending Greetings from a New View

Directions: Be honest and consider a cultural or social group that you believe you may have a difficult time counseling or have a hard time understanding. Alternatively, think of a place you avoid. In identifying a group or place, you might think of a cultural population, a group of people with different viewpoints or experiences than your own, or a place where you feel discomfort. Pretend that you visited this group or place and write a postcard to a friend or family member in the space provided to describe your experience. If necessary, do some research on the group or place you identify. Write about your feelings and thoughts about the visit, as well as questions and new insights that might come up for you during your time with this group or in this location. Use the space provided on the back if necessary.

Processing: Sending Greetings from a New View

What informed your decision to visit the group or location you identified?

_____

_____

_____

_____

_____

_____

What will you need to be aware of, regarding your feelings and thoughts, when counseling members of this group?

_____

_____

_____

_____

_____

_____

Where, or when, have you experienced discomfort related to a bias this week?

Who could you reach out to, or what would you need to do, in order to increase your comfort working with this population?

_____

_____

_____

_____

_____

_____

What are the strengths of this group, and what can you learn from working with its members?

_____

_____

_____

_____

_____

_____

How will your ability to work well with this group improve your professional identity?

_____

_____

_____

_____

_____

_____

Taking It to the Group

- What feelings did group members experience when members shared their postcards?

- Provide feedback and insight to one another in supportive and empathic ways. For example, is there a member in the group that represents the population written about or a member who has comfort working with the population?

- In what ways can counselors ensure empathy and unconditional positive regard to all clients?

- Share resources that can be helpful in expanding multicultural and social awareness surrounding the populations or social groups discussed in this activity.

- Why are competency models related to working with marginalized groups important for counselors? How do they relate to counseling professional identity?

My additional thoughts and feelings about the
Sending Greetings from a New View **activity...**

Supervisor Reflections

Follow-up Supervision Group Activities

- Bring MSJCC (Ratts et al., 2016), the LGBQQIA counseling competencies (ALGBTIC, 2013) and the Competencies for Counseling Transgender Clients (AGBTIC, 2010) to class. Discuss reasons why competencies, such as these, are important for professional counseling.

- Create a set of competencies relevant to populations identified in this activity. Further, consider the existing multicultural and social justice competencies, LGBTQQIA, and transgender competencies to determine if any additions or updates might be necessary.

- Research laws or injustices that impact marginalized populations and write a letter or make a phone call to local or national representatives on their behalf.

References

Ahmed, S., Wilson, K. B., Henriksen, R. C., Jr., & Jones, J. W. (2011). What does it mean to be a culturally-competence counselor? *Journal for Social Action in Counseling and Psychology*, *3*(1), 17–28.

ALGBTIC. (2010). American Counseling Association competencies for counseling with transgender clients. *Journal of LGBT Issues in Counseling*, *4*(3), 135–159. doi:10.1080/15538605.2010.524839

American Counseling Association. (2014). *Code of ethics*. Retrieved from www.counseling.org/resources/aca-code-of-ethics.pdf

American Counseling Association. (2018). *Advocacy competencies*. Retrieved from www.counseling.org/docs/default-source/competencies/aca-2018-advocacy-competencies.pdf?sfvrsn=1dca552c_6

Atkins, S. L., Fitzpatrick, M. R., Poolokasingham, G., Lebeau, M., & Spanierman, L. B. (2017). Make it personal: A qualitative investigation of white counselors' multicultural awareness development. *The Counseling Psychologist*, *45*(5), 669–696. doi:10.1177/0011000017719458

Cashwell, C. S., & Watts, R. E. (2010). The new ASERVIC competencies for addressing spiritual and religious issues in counseling. *Counseling and Values*, *55*, 2–5. doi:10.1002/j.2161-007X.2010.tb00018.x

Chan, C. D., Cor, D. N., & Band, M. P. (2018). Privilege and oppression in counselor education: An intersectionality framework. *Journal of Multicultural Counseling and Development*, *46*(1), 58–73. doi:10.1002/jmcd.12092

Council for Accreditation of Counseling and Related Educational Programs. (2016). *CACREP accreditation standards and procedures manual*. Alexandria, VA: Author.

Daksun. (2019). White isolated mask on black background with neutral facial expression [JPEG]. Retrieved from www.shutterstock.com/image-photo/white-isolated-mask-on-black-background-1403100044

Estrada, D., Poulsen, S., Cannon, E., & Wiggins, M. (2013). Orienting counseling students toward multiculturalism: Exploring privilege during a new student orientation. *Journal of Humanistic Counseling*, *52*(1), 80–91. doi:10.1002/j.2161-1939.2013.00034.x

Gutierrez, D., & Mullen, P. R. (2016). Emotional intelligence and the counselor: Examining the relationship of trait emotional intelligence to counselor burnout. *Journal of Mental Health Counseling*, *38*(3), 187–200. doi:10.1774/mehc.38.3.01

Harper, A., Finnerty, P., Martinez, M., Brace, A., Crethar, H. C., Loos, B., & Hammer, T. (2013). Association for Lesbian, Gay, Bisexual, and Transgender Issues in Counseling competencies for counseling with lesbian, gay, bisexual, queer, questioning, intersex, and ally individuals. *Journal of LGBT Issues in Counseling*, *7*(1), 2–43. doi:10.1080/15538605.2013.755444

Hliv, A. (2019). Man standing outline [JPEG]. Retrieved from www.shutterstock.com/image-illustration/man-standing-outline-flat-cartoon-icon-519914833

Hook, J. N., Davis, D. E., Owen, J., Worthington, E. L., Jr., & Utsey, S. O. (2013). Cultural humility: Measuring openness to culturally diverse clients. *Journal of Counseling Psychology*, *60*(3), 353–366. doi:10.1037/a0032595

Lewis, J. A., Ratts, M. J., Paladino, D. A., & Toporek, R. L. (2011). Social justice counseling and advocacy: Developing new leadership roles and competencies. *Journal of Social Action in Counseling and Psychology*, *3*(1), 5–16.

Matthews, J. J., Barden, S. J., & Sherrell, R. S. (2018). Examining the relationships between multicultural counseling competence, multicultural self-efficacy, and ethnic identity development of practicing counselors. *Journal of Mental Health Counseling*, *40*(2), 129–141. doi:10.17744/mehc.40.2.03

Ratts, M. J., & Greenleaf, A. T. (2018). Counselor-advocate-scholar model: Changing the dominant discourse in counseling. *Journal of Multicultural Counseling and Development*, *46*(2), 78–96. doi:10.1002/jmcd.12094

Ratts, M. J., Singh, A. A., Nassar-McMillan, S., Butler, S. K., & McCullough, J. R. (2016). Multicultural and social justice counseling competencies: Guidelines for the counseling profession. *Journal of Multicultural Counseling and Development*, *44*(1), 28–48. doi:10.1002/jmcd.12035

Shannonhouse, L. R., Barden, S., & Mobley, A. K. (2015). Qualitative outcomes of a homestay immersion with critical reflection. *Counselor Education and Supervision*, *54*(4), 302–319. doi:10.1002/ceas.12028

Shannonhouse, L. R., & West-Olatunji, C. (2013, Winter). One counselor-trainee's journey toward multicultural counseling competence: The role of mentoring in executing intentional cultural immersion. *Professional Issues in Counseling*. Retrieved from: www.shsu.edu/~piic/documents/OneCounselorTrainee%E2%80%99sJourneyToward MulticulturalCounselingCompetence.pdf

Sue, D. W., Torino, G. C., Capodilupo, C. M., Rivera, D. P., & Lin, A. I. (2009). How white faculty perceive and react to difficult dialogues on race: Implications for education and training. *The Counseling Psychologist*, *37*(8), 1090–1115. doi:10.1177/0011000009340443

CHAPTER 6

THEORETICAL ORIENTATION

Theory provides counselors with framework and structure to conceptualize and treat clients (Halbur & Halbur, 2015). Theory is useful from assessment to termination as it provides explanation for the human condition, the etiology of a problem, and how to facilitate change. Counseling theories also have related skills and interventions that can be used in sessions with the purpose of catalyzing the change process. Finally, theory can guide how counselors present in sessions (e.g., directive, collaborative, teaching) and provide an indication of how clients engage in the process (e.g., lead the session, be an expert, or be educated by the counselor).

Counselor professional identity scholars have suggested that choosing a counseling theory is related to professional identity (Calley & Hawley, 2008; Moss, Gibson, & Dollarhide, 2014). Though there is no evidence that professional counselors endorse different theories than their helping profession counterparts (e.g., psychologists, social workers), Barth and Moody (2019) determined that strength-based and solution-focused theories were reported more frequently in their investigation of American Mental Health Counselor Association counselors' use of theory, as opposed to similar past studies in psychology. Though their data also included cognitive behavioral and humanistic theories, they speculated the high number of strength-based and solution-focused theories may be a reflection of counseling philosophy as more than half of their sample were educated in CACREP programs. In their diagnosis and treatment planning textbook, Kress and Paylo (2019) also emphasized the importance of counselors adopting a strength-based counseling approach when working with clients. They suggested that counselors look for clients' strengths when considering treatment techniques and built this focus into their conceptualization and treatment-planning model. Further, Myers and Sweeney's (2005) book outlined the importance of counselors adopting a wellness and developmental perspective when working with clients, as did Ohrt, Clarke, and Conley (2019) as they promoted a wellness and prevention lens when counseling clients across the lifespan in their textbook.

Alongside strength-based and wellness models, humanistic theories have also been linked to professional counselors' work. Dollarhide and Oliver (2014) reasoned that humanistic values (e.g., self-actualization; responsibility; holism; innate goodness; and counselor qualities of empathy, unconditional positive regard, and congruence as a means for change) inherently fit well with the philosophical tenets of counseling. Calley and Hawley (2008) provided evidence for this through their inquiry into the professional identity of counselor educators, in which the majority of participants ascribed to either humanistic or constructivist theories. Further, when Luke and Goodrich (2010) studied the professional identity of Chi Sigma Iota leaders, they also found humanistic, as well as developmental, philosophies as influential belief systems held by their participants.

Though strength-based, wellness, and humanistic models of counseling may be well matched with the philosophical tenets of counseling, professional counselors use a wide array of theories. As ascribing to a counseling theory is an essential part of being a counselor, it is an important learning objective for the Council of Accreditation of Counseling and Related Programs (Section 2.F.5.a; Section 3; 2016). As such, counselor education programs include course work about theories and their associated skills. Later in their education, during practicum and internship, counselor trainees are afforded time to apply and practice their skills in different theories while under supervision. There are hundreds of theories to work from and counselor educators are tasked with choosing which to include in their curriculum. Ultimately, students might learn common counseling theories (e.g., Psychodynamic, Adlerian, Existential, Person-Centered, Experiential, CBT, Reality Therapy, REBT, Solution-Focused, Narrative, Feminist) and be asked to select a theory they like best or one that fits well with their own beliefs to further endorse.

Finding this sense of authenticity when selecting a model can be essential in building a therapeutic relationship with a client. Counseling outcomes are more successful when counselors are able to build an alliance, in which they are empathic, show unconditional positive regard, and are genuine (Wampold, 2015). If counselors select a theory they believe in and that aligns with their own assumptions or experiences, they may be more likely to use it naturally and consistently and in turn feel more genuine in sessions. Therefore, counselors should consider how to be genuine with their choice of theory. As theory is directly related to the interventions and skills counselors use in session (Barth & Moody, 2019), adhering to an authentic theoretical framework throughout the counseling relationship is important. Therefore, counselors should consider how to be genuine with their choice of theory. This requires self-reflection of one's beliefs about counseling and the change process, as well as the exploration of abilities and strengths.

Scholars have made suggestions about how to facilitate a learning process that encourages counselor trainees to find a personal theory and philosophy of counseling. As theory choice is influenced by counselors' personal philosophies, beliefs, and values (Bitar, Bean, & Bermudez, 2007), as well as their cognitive and emotional styles (Barrio Minton & Myers, 2008; Powell & Newgent, 2011; Worthington & Dillon, 2003), counselor trainees are also expected to engage in self-reflection as they learn theory and counseling models. Spruill and Benshoff (2000) suggested a three-phase process in which students (a) explore their personal values and beliefs that lead them to a career in counseling, (b) study counseling theories in order to integrate them with their own beliefs, and (c) practice a variety of counseling theories in practicum and internship in an effort to formulate a personal theory of counseling. Guiffrida (2005) also suggested students embrace their existing knowledge and natural instincts as they learn counseling theories. His model invites students to naturally engage in interventions and techniques and use self-reflection to link their practice to counseling theory.

Over time, and as students learn more about theory, students' ideas might also evolve and shift. Throughout an introductory theory course, researchers identified that students' pre-existing ideas about theory expand and develop over time, suggesting that exposure to theoretical assumptions and conversations will cause shifts in ideation from the beginning to the end of a course (Hinkle, Schermer, & Beasley, 2015). These findings suggested that though reflection on pre-existing knowledge and innate qualities related to counseling theory is important, providing space for growth due to new experiences and information is also warranted. This supports conclusions other researchers found that suggested education, experience, and supervision are additional facets that impact theory choice (Poznanski & McLennan, 2003). As such, continued exploration and exposure to theories is important, as is engaging in conversations about theories and applying them in various ways.

After learning theories, more advanced counselors may also choose to work from multiple theories. Barth and Moody's (2019) study also revealed that counselors are influenced by many theories simultaneously. Though they cautioned against identifying this as being eclectic or integrative, they indicated this could be a future trend to consider. This supports a past recommendation that counselor trainees learn theories via "the ways paradigm" (Cheston, 2000), in which students learn theories' ways of being, understanding, and intervening in an effort to appreciate how different theories might be grouped together. Corey (2019) also provides counselors ideas on how to group together counseling theories in an effort to be more integrative.

Being familiar with theory also helps counselors to examine them more critically and even determine how they can be adapted to better suit clients (Stiles, 2007). For example, Benish, Quintana, and Wampold (2011) indicated the importance of adapting theory to culture in order to be a more culturally responsive counselor. Brubaker, Puig, Reese, and Young (2010) also stressed the importance of critically examining theories in order to use them in ways that promote social justice. They suggested students discussing how cultural values influenced theory development, and how the ways in which they integrate their own beliefs and assumptions can be further oppressive or liberating. Brubaker et al. (2010) encouraged students learning to use theory in ways that promote community and consider their use on a larger perspective. Regardless, counselors are expected to be critical of the theories and skills they use and consider creative ways to make adaption in order to be a more culturally responsive and socially just counselor.

Exploration of theory is a critical component of counselor education, and choosing a theory to work from is a task related to counselor professional identity development. Theories and skills related to humanism, strengths and solutions, wellness, and development aligns well with the philosophical underpinnings of counseling. Professional counselors, though, have the freedom to ascribe to any counseling theory that fits and works well for them, which can lead to a more authentic presentation in sessions.

Connecting Theoretical Orientation to You

The activities in this chapter can help you explore the importance of using theory when working with clients as a way to promote your professional identity. Throughout the assignments you are asked to consider the valuable information and direction theories can provide a counselor when working with a client. This serves as a useful reminder that professional counselors should have therapeutic intent as they aim to help clients alleviate their presenting problems. This therapeutic intent indicates that anything you do during sessions should have meaning. Often this can be related to, and grounded in, theory.

Activities include exploring your beliefs about the counseling process, as well as the change process. For example, counselors might choose to spend more or less time discussing the past versus future depending on what they consider to be important in helping clients. Considering facets that stimulate change is also important. Does the impetus for change require shifting cognitions, emotional awareness, relearning behaviors, changing dialogue about a problem, or, perhaps, something else? The answer to this question can lead you to identifying a focus of counseling in order to reach therapeutic change. For example, if you believe that change comes through emotional awareness, you might spend much of a session exploring feelings on a conscious and unconscious level. Counselors who take time to reflect about what they believe is critical to spend time on in sessions can be more intentional in their work. This is part of the integrative process of professional identity, during which you examine how your beliefs, abilities, and skills contribute to your unique demonstration of professional identity.

Finally, you are asked to consider your unique legacy in using or changing a theory. As traditional theories might have room for improvement with diverse populations or to meet needs of our current society, counselors can find creative ways to demonstrate theory. How might you make a unique mark on a counseling theory? How can your distinct uses of theory work to promote the philosophy of professional counseling and be an extension of your professional identity? Ultimately, upon completion of this chapter you will explore the importance of, alignment to, and your potential contributions and adaptations toward theory while considering your professional identity.

Activity 21: Theory Road Map

Directions: Counseling and human development theories provide structure in conceptualizing and facilitating treatment for clients. Illustrate the map on this page (front and back) with road signs, conditions, or other ideas (e.g., speed bumps, animal crossings) to show how theory can guide work with clients from the beginning through the termination of a counseling relationship. Rather than using a particular theory to formulate your map, think of this in terms of the usefulness of having any theory in mind. For example, rather than specific theoretical tenets, consider how all theories work to inform the counselor on facilitating sessions (e.g., it can inform a counselor how to build a relationship with a client, how directive to be in session, and inform techniques) and how counselors might feel "lost" or on a "road to nowhere" without a theory in mind.

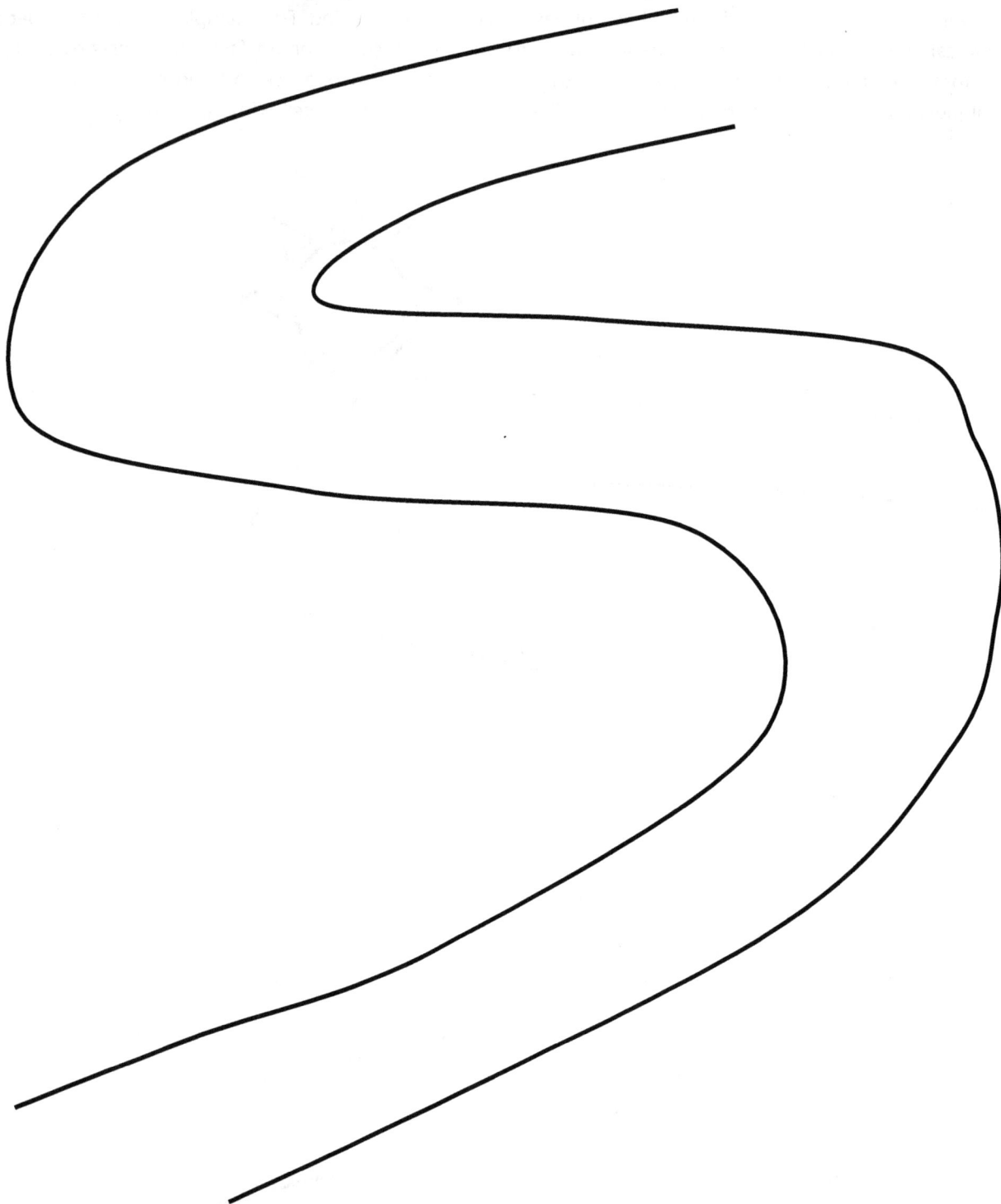

Processing: Theory Road Map

In reviewing your map, summarize how theory is a useful aspect of counseling and why it is important for counselors to adopt?

_____

_____

_____

_____

_____

_____

How does theory guide counseling and what might be repercussions for not using theory?

_____

_____

_____

_____

_____

_____

_____

When has theory guided you this week?

What is your favorite illustration added to the map? How does it represent an important reason for using theory when counseling?

_____

_____

_____

_____

_____

_____

What if there was an unexpected road construction sign in this "theory roadway"? What might this mean and what would you do to avoid danger?

_____

_____

_____

_____

_____

_____

Aside from facilitating counseling sessions and structuring work with clients, what other circumstance might a professional counselor be informed by theory?

_____

_____

_____

_____

_____

_____

Taking It to the Group

- What was a common theme among the group regarding the importance of theory for guiding a counselor's work?

- Now that everyone has shared their maps, is there anything additional that the group thought of that would be important to add?

- Aside from theory, what other concepts or skills guide sessions and inform the counselor?

- What advice would the group give to a new counselor who said that theory was not important?

- Before learning about specific counseling or human development theories, what does the group believe is important for counselor trainees to grasp about the importance of theory?

My additional thoughts and feelings about the
Theory Road Map **activity...**

Supervisor Reflections

Follow-up Supervision Group Activities

- Based on group members' maps, further discuss the usefulness of theory by creating a Top 10 List of why theory is important in professional counseling.

- Create some catchy rhymes that fit with the story told by the group members' theory maps that remind counselors of the importance of using theory when working with clients.

- Interview supervisors or other counselors on the importance of using theory in their work. Report back findings to the group.

Activity 22: Metaphor for Change

Directions: Counseling theories provide ideas to implement change and help clients achieve their counseling goals. Each theory describes tenets on why problems exist and how people can make changes in order to eliminate presenting problems. Consider your own beliefs and experiences. What do you believe creates change for a person? In the space below illustrate, write, list song lyrics, or paste a photograph to serve as a metaphor that represents your belief of the change process.

Processing: Metaphor for Change

Describe your metaphor for change.

_____

_____

_____

_____

_____

_____

Why is it important for counselors to consider their beliefs about change when exploring theory?

_____

_____

_____

_____

_____

_____

How have you experienced change this week?

Apply your metaphor to a time when you have experienced a change and describe the connection below.

_____

_____

_____

_____

_____

_____

How does applying your experience with change to the metaphor help you process your experience in a new way?

_____

_____

_____

_____

_____

_____

_____

How does metaphor help make difficult concepts clearer?

_____

_____

_____

_____

_____

_____

Taking It to the Group

- What were some themes that emerged as the group shared their metaphors for change?

- What contributing factors led to everyone's beliefs about change and how might these beliefs evolve, or stay consistent, over time?

- Knowing everyone's beliefs about the change process, how can the group be more informed to offer peer-supervision?

- How are metaphors useful in conveying messages about difficult concepts? What other times does the group believe they could be useful?

- When considering the beliefs of the counseling profession, what might be some shared assumptions about change built within counseling professional identity?

My additional thoughts and feelings about the
Metaphor for Change **activity...**

Supervisor Reflections

Follow-up Supervision Group Activities

- When is change difficult? Share times when members had a hard time making change. Talk about the process of overcoming this difficulty.

- Discuss the definition and philosophical underpinnings of counseling and create a metaphor that could depict an *atheoretical* (or not associated with theory) perspective of change that represents counseling.

- Create a group metaphor to describe the change process that members experience as they develop into new counselors. This metaphor can be used throughout group supervision when helping group members conceptualize their work with difficult clients or navigating professional issues.

Activity 23: Theory Fill-in-the-Blank

Directions: Choosing a counseling theory is an important part of being a counselor. Theory guides counselors to understanding why a presenting problem exists and provides ideas on how to facilitate change in order to eradicate the problem. The interventions and techniques associated with theory aim to catalyze this change. Finally, theory also guides counselors in how to present in a counseling session and how to set up a therapeutic rapport. For this activity, consider your beliefs about the etiology of problems, goals of counseling, facilitating change, and the general tone of counseling sessions. Answer the numbered statements below and then turn the page over to fill your answers in the respective blank spaces.

1. Presenting problem:

2. What a client might want as a result of counseling:

3. Two characteristics of a counselor:

4. Something a counselor would want to learn about from a client:

5. Something to talk about with a client in order to learn what is listed in #4:

6. Problems for clients exist when:

7. A therapeutic goal of counseling that would facilitate change:

8. Two skills a counselor might use in session:

9. Important information for a counselor to listen to as a client talks about him/herself:

10. Something a client might talk about in relation to the presenting problem listed above:

11. A therapeutic intervention to work on in relation to #7:

12. Therapeutic rationale for the intervention listed in #8:

13. Something a client needs to do during counseling in order to create change:

14. A therapeutic gain a client will make in counseling to indicate personal growth and change:

15. Restate presenting problem listed in #1:

16. Why the presenting problem listed in #1 is no longer a problem after successful counseling:

Theory Fill-in-the-Blank

Monica came to counseling because _____ and she wanted
1

_____. When first meeting with her, I aimed to be
2

_____ and _____. I wanted to learn
3　　　　　　　　　　　　　　　3

about _____ so I made statements and asked questions related to
4

_____. After hearing more from her and learning what lead her to
5

counseling and what she wanted out of coming, I realized she was likely experiencing this presenting

problem because _____. In order for her to achieve her goals she
6

would benefit from _____. Throughout our session I
7

_____ and _____. I listened closely to
8　　　　　　　　　　　　　　　8

what she was telling me, which was important so I could identify _____.
9

At one point she discussed _____, and I realized that the intervention
10

_____ would be important so that she _____.
11　　　　　　　　　　　　　　　12

As counseling continued, I used more interventions like this in hopes she would _____.
13

After multiple sessions, Monica showed growth. She _____.
14

By the end of counseling, Monica's goals for counseling were met and she improved

_____. She was able to achieve this improvement because, ultimately
15

_____.
16

Processing: Theory Fill-in-the-Blank

How does your Fill-in-the-Blank story fit, or not fit, your beliefs about the focus of counseling sessions and how to facilitate therapeutic change?

_____

_____

_____

_____

_____

_____

If necessary, change the sentences or phrases in the story to better reflect your theoretical beliefs. Summarize some of the changes in the space below to more accurately articulate your beliefs.

_____

_____

_____

_____

_____

_____

In what ways have you experienced the importance of theory this week?

Though you were not instructed to use a specific counseling theory to complete this project, read your story with counseling theories in mind. What theory do you believe is most accurately reflected in your story?

_____

_____

_____

_____

_____

_____

Is the theory you identified in the previous question reflected in a consistent and accurate way? Are all of the theory tenets congruent with one another (e.g., the cause of a problem, the beliefs about change, and techniques are aligned to one theory)? Explain.

_____

_____

_____

_____

_____

_____

How does this activity illustrate the importance of choosing one theoretical home to work from, or perhaps two theories that have similar philosophical tenets, as opposed to not having a theoretical base?

_____

_____

_____

_____

_____

_____

Taking It to the Group

- As a group, decide how well members' stories align with particular theories.

- What did the group learn about the importance of using theory to guide work with clients?

- How can group members continue to work toward theory development and support one another during group supervision in achieving the goal of exploring theory?

- How would the group help other counselors regarding finding a theory to consistently use? In what ways might some of the traditional theories need to be changed in order to align with the philosophical tenets of counseling?

My additional thoughts and feelings about the
Theory Fill-in-the-Blank **activity...**

Supervisor Reflections

Follow-up Supervision Group Activities

- Are there benefits to using one theory, or should counselors be more integrative or eclectic? Devise a "pros and cons" list related to the idea of picking one theory to work from versus using many different theories.

- Use the format of the story in this activity, and apply the idea to case presentations during supervision. When doing so, align the story to the group member's preferred theory.

- Interview other counselors about their sessions to determine how they are using theory. Find out how they came to find their theoretical match or home base.

Activity 24: The Theory of You

Directions: We hope our work has impact. This impact may be small and direct to one person or a few clients. The impact could also be much larger to the field of professional counseling. For this activity, think about potential impact you can have through your unique use of counseling theory. Think about how you fit with the theory of your choice and consider changes you might make to it or ways that you would use it that would have a lasting impression long after you retire. How would you want people to describe your contribution to the theory? Alternatively, consider creating a new theory that people can use. There are so many ways to consider your potential impact on counseling theories (e.g., an emergent theory, specific technique, multicultural contributions to a theory, updating it to current issues, webinars, practice video series, conferences dedicated to the theory).

Processing: The Theory of You

How did you start to think of what you wanted your legacy of theory to be?

_____

_____

_____

_____

_____

_____

As you started writing about your theoretical contributions, what seemed to be the most important aspects to include? What sparked your interest and what did you want to share with others as you created a legacy?

_____

_____

_____

_____

_____

_____

Where have you experienced your legacy this week?

Do you feel that your work can make a contribution to the field of professional counseling? If so, in what ways? If not, how else might you make a contribution to the field?

_____

_____

_____

_____

_____

_____

Is there any way you could accomplish what you wrote? If so, how would you start?

_____

_____

_____

_____

_____

_____

What would the direct impact to the use of theory be because of your contribution?

_____

_____

_____

_____

_____

_____

Taking It to the Group

- Allow group members to share their contributions. Go in a circle, and provide time for each group member to ask a question to expand the theoretical legacy each member is creating.

- Spend time discussing the connection between each person in the group and the unique way they are creating a legacy through their chosen, or emergent, theory. What is the hidden message in their goals? Are there ways that they can move towards their larger goals during their practicum or internship experience?

- What legacy does the group want to leave behind for future practicum and internships students?

- What is some advice to give to emerging counselors to develop their theoretical orientation and the importance it holds to professional identity?

- How does the advancement of theoretical orientations, or adapting theory to meet the needs of a current society, help to move the field into the future?

My additional thoughts and feelings about the
Theory of You activity...

Supervisor Reflections

Follow-up Supervision Group Activities

- Reflect on personal or professional experiences that impacted each member's future goals and the contributions they want to make through their work.

- Create a Top Ten List of counseling theorists, or other leaders in the field, and their most profound contributions to counseling.

- Work as a group to create one contribution your group can provide to the counseling profession. Identify the ways each group member can use their strengths to work towards leaving behind this legacy.

References

Barrio Minton, C. A., & Myers, J. E. (2008). Cognitive style and theoretical orientation: Factors affecting intervention style interest and use. *Journal of Mental Health Counseling, 30,* 330–344. doi:10.17744/mehc.30.4.5626315033866460

Barth, A. L., & Moody, S. J. (2019). Theory use in counseling practice: Current trends. *International Journal for the Advancement of Counselling.* doi:10.1007/s10447-018- 9352-0

Benish, S. G., Quintana, S., & Wampold, B. E. (2011). Culturally adapted psychotherapy and the legitimacy of myth: A direct-comparison meta-analysis. *Journal of Counseling Psychology, 58,* 279–289. doi:10.1037/a0023626

Bitar, G. W., Bean, R. A., & Bermudez, J. M. (2007). Influences and processes in theoretical orientation development: A grounded theory pilot study. *The American Journal of Family Therapy, 35,* 109–121. doi:10.1080/01926180600553407

Brubaker, M. D., Puig, A., Reese, R. F., & Young, J. (2010). Integrating social justice into counseling theories pedagogy: A case example. *Counselor Education and Supervision, 50,* 88–102. doi:10.1002/j.1556-6978.2010.tb00111.x

Calley, N. G., & Hawley, L. D. (2008). The professional identity of counselor educators. *The Clinical Supervisor, 27*(1), 3–16. doi:10.1080/07325220802221454

Cheston, S. E. (2000). A new paradigm for teaching counseling theory and practice. *Counselor Education and Supervision, 39,* 254–269. doi:10.1002/j.1556-6978.2000.tb01236.x

Corey, G. (2019). *The art of integrative counseling* (4th ed.). Alexandria, VA: American Counseling Association.

Council for Accreditation of Counseling and Related Educational Programs. (2016). *CACREP accreditation standards and procedures manual.* Alexandria, VA: Author.

Dollarhide, C. T., & Oliver, K. (2014). Humanistic professional identity: The transtheoretical tie that binds. *Journal of Humanistic Counseling, 53*(3), 203–217. doi:10.1002/j.2161-1939.2014.00057.x

Guiffrida, D. A. (2005). The emergence model: An alternative pedagogy for facilitating self-reflection and theoretical fit in counseling students. *Counselor Education and Supervision, 44,* 201–213. doi:10.1002/j.1556-6978.2005.tb01747.x

Halbur, D., & Halbur, K. V. (2015). *Developing your own theoretical orientation in counseling and psychotherapy* (3rd ed.). Boston, MA: Pearson.

Hinkle, M. S., Schermer, T. W., & Beasley, K. (2015). Student theoretical beliefs at the beginning and end of a counseling theories course. *Journal of Counselor Practice, 6*(1), 6–21. doi:10.22229/tbs019653

Kress, V. E., & Paylo, M. J. (2019). *Treating those with mental disorders: A comprehensive approach to case conceptualization and treatment* (2nd ed.). New York, NY: Pearson.

Luke, M., & Goodrich, K. M. (2010). Chi Sigma Iota chapter leadership and professional identity development in early career counselors. *Counselor Education and Supervision, 50,* 56–78. doi:10.1002/j.1556-6978.2010.tb00108.x

Moss, J. M., Gibson, D. M., & Dollarhide, C. T. (2014). Professional identity development: A grounded theory of transformational tasks of counselors. *Journal of Counseling & Development, 92,* 3–12. doi:10.1002/j.1556-6676.2014.00124.x

Myers, J. E., & Sweeney, T. J. (2005). *Counseling for wellness: Theory research and practice.* Alexandria, VA: American Counseling Association.

Ohrt, J. H., Clarke, P. B., & Conley, A. H. (2019). *Wellness counseling: A holistic approach to prevention and intervention.* Alexandria, VA: American Counseling Association.

Powell, M. L., & Newgent, R. A. (2011). Assertiveness in mental health professionals: Differences between insight-oriented and action-oriented clinicians. *The Professional Counseling, 1*(2), 92–98. doi:10.15241/mlp.1.2.92

Poznanski, J. J., & McLennan, J. (2003). Becoming a psychologist with a particular theoretical orientation to counselling practice. *Australian Psychologist, 38*(3), 223–226. doi:10.1080/00050060310001707247

Spruill, D. A., & Benshoff, J. M. (2000). Helping beginning counselors develop a personal theory of counseling. *Counselor Education and Supervision, 40,* 70–80. doi:10.1002/j.1556-6978.2000.tbt01800.x

Stiles, W. B. (2007). Theory-building case studies of counseling and psychotherapy. *Counselling and Psychotherapy Research, 7*(2), 122–127. doi:10.1080/14733140701356742

Wampold, B. E. (2015). How important are the common factors in psychotherapy? An update. *World Psychiatry, 14*(3), 270–277. doi:10.1002/wps.20238

Worthington, R. L., & Dillon, F. R. (2003). The theoretical orientation profile scale revisited: A validation study. *Measurement and Evaluation in Counseling and Development, 36,* 95–105. doi:10.1177/0748175616664005

CHAPTER 7

PERSONAL AND PROFESSIONAL VALUES

The definition of values has changed over the years throughout the counseling profession (Bridges, Hicks, Lazzo, & Keegan, 2019). Cottone and Tarvydas (2016) defined values to "involve that which is intrinsically worthwhile … values reflect the holder's worldview, culture, or understanding of the world" (p. 40). This definition includes the moral component of values that are guiding ethical principles and determine good from bad, right from wrong, or permissible from nonpermissible. ACA (2014) notes that "professional values are an important way of living out an ethical commitment" (p. 3), which is an important part of professional identity.

The concept of values has evolved over time to include more than moral beliefs of holders and extends to one's preferences, including nonmoral beliefs (Cottone & Tarvydas, 2016). Nonmoral beliefs include health, education, or personal preferences. Bridges et al. (2019) noted that values are in a state of constant flux and are subject to change as members in society evolve and interact with others. The impact of communication on society has shown to shift individuals' values.

As counselor trainees, the understanding of one's own values is critical to the counseling field (Moss, Gibson, & Dollarhide, 2014). There is evidence that adhering to shared values that are related to the professional counseling field (i.e., respect, diversity awareness, and confidentiality) improve client outcomes (Dollarhide, 2013). These values may be considered nonmoral and there are ways to develop teaching these skills in counselor education academic programs that can improve skills in counselor trainees (Dollarhide, 2013). Corey, Corey, Corey, and Callanan (2015) identified "bracketing," the need for counselors to prevent their own values from negatively influencing the therapeutic process, as important (p. 70). Therefore, supporting ACA Code of Ethics (2014) which charges professional counselors to be respectful of differences; counselors should avoid imposing personal values on clients; and, above all, do no harm (Standard A.4.).

Researchers examined moral development and personal values and found they were the most significant predictor of professional ethical identity formation, meaning that a counselor's professional values served as a guiding light in ethical dilemmas (Lloyd-Hazlett & Foster, 2017). These values intersect with other counseling components, such as advocacy and support work with clients (Crethar & Winterowd, 2012; Levitt & Aligo, 2013; Young, Dollarhide, & Baughman, 2015). Research also found counselors who developed ways of forgiveness as part of their own values, were shown to be impactful on wellness and moral identity (Moorhead, Gill, Minton, & Myers, 2012). The integration of professional and personal worldviews is an integral part of counselor professional identity development (Gibson, Dollarhide, & Moss, 2010). There are specific values that need to be taught to counselors, as these values are standards in the field. Bloom, McNeil, Flasch, and Sanders (2018) examined the skill of empathy and the need to develop the skill and value of it into the counseling identity of counselor trainees. Levitt and Aligo (2013) examined ethical decision making, moral orientation, and the role these have in how counselors make decisions in situations that present ethical conflicts, including counselor trainees recognizing the need for training and foundation in professional understanding and practice.

The concept of professional and personal values is not new to professional counselors. This is an area that has been discussed throughout research and is incorporated into the American Counseling Association (2014) and supported by CACREP (2016, Section 2.F.2). The importance of understanding one's own values, has been demonstrated as necessary to engage in professional counseling with clients (Moss et al., 2014). There are direct connections to positive client outcomes for those professional counselors who identified, explored, reflected, and examined their own personal values to ensure that these were not imparted on the client (Bridges et al., 2019). The definition that Cottone and Tarvydas (2016) created recognizes the difference between values of moral components and those of nonmoral, yet the exploration of both are equally important. As such, these values really go beyond moral decisions and look at personal concepts, such as forgiveness, respect, communication, leadership, and advocacy skills. As counselors, it is important to reflect on personal feelings and their connection to personal values, and then the intersection with your professional values. There is evidence that one's personal beliefs regarding forgiveness in their personal lives actually had a positive impact on their wellness, which is then imparted to work with clients (Moorhead et al., 2012). It has also been seen that the role of advocacy as a value in counselor's work was important for successful counselors (Young et al., 2015) and is needed to incorporate into their personal and professional values as there is a positive impact for the clients and a commitment from the counseling profession (Crethar & Winterowd, 2012).

Connecting Personal and Professional Values to You

As you continue to travel along your journey to becoming a counseling professional, it is essential to examine your values, including your professional values, to ensure that all are ethically compliant (ACA, 2014). The activities included in this chapter push you to identify different areas in your development, which impact what you believe and how you see the world and potentially other individuals. This view of the world can impact the work you do with clients and if left unexamined can have a potential negative impact on them. Research has defined values as more than beliefs or bias and recognized that it changes with more exposure and communication with others and society. This helps to challenge thoughts and move to different spaces of our development and understanding. The activities will help you to look at different aspects of yourself and then help you to determine areas where you can further reflect. As you reflect on different parts of yourself and your worldview, this is translated to the view of clients. Most of our values support and help clients by establishing a secure therapeutic alliance, providing the space clients need to examine themselves. Continuing to address our values ensures the best interest of our clients continues to be our priority.

Activity 25: Connect Your Values

Directions: We know that our personal values should not negatively impede our professional ones but in order to do this we must be aware of our values and their potential to influence our work. To begin this activity, choose one color marker or pen and list your personal values under "Personal." Do the same thing for "Professional" values, but with a different color marker or pen. Once you complete these two tasks, follow the rest of the directions below.

PERSONAL   **PROFESSIONAL**

After completing each list, draw a line between the Personal and Professional values that are, or are almost, the same.

Now list the remaining values here. Those remaining should be the values that do not overlap between the personal and professional values listed above. Use the original color maker or pen when listing the value so that you can match the value with being either "personal" or "professional" above.

VALUES

Processing: Connect Your Values

How did you identify your personal values?

_____

_____

_____

_____

_____

_____

How did you identify your professional values?

_____

_____

_____

_____

_____

_____

Where have you experienced conflicts with your values this week?

As you looked at those connected, what themes emerged?

_____

_____

_____

_____

_____

_____

What was it like to identify the values that did not connect? Reflect on those left on the bottom list.

_____

_____

_____

_____

_____

_____

From your last list, do you foresee any instances where your personal and professional values may result in conflict?

_____

_____

_____

_____

_____

_____

Taking It to the Group

- We know that our values have an impact on our professional work. Talk about what this may mean, including benefits and pitfalls.

- What are some values that the group holds and how does this help the group work well together?

- Do group members have any conflicting values or beliefs about counseling? If so, how do group members work together amidst this difference? How does the group benefit from different perspectives?

- What is some advice that the group might offer to new counselors entering the field regarding the relationship between your personal values and professional values?

- What resources does the profession provide for helping professional counselors maintain counseling competencies when working with clients who might hold different values?

My additional thoughts and feelings about the *Connect Your Values* activity...

Supervisor Reflections

Follow-up Supervision Group Activities

- As group members share some of their values, create a list of any values that evokes an emotional response in another group member.

- As a group, work together to identify ways members can investigate other opportunities to understand their own values and the impact it has on their work. Brainstorm opportunities for growth and exploration.

- Allow each group member the space to share any values that they may be struggling with. Spend time discussing values that we hold, yet we hide from others. What are the implications of this in our work with clients?

Activity 26: Celebrity Role Model

Directions: Having someone to look up to is not just for kids! Consider a role model or hero in your life who you admire. The person may have similar values to you or it might be someone you strive to be like. Though you likely have role models in your family or circle of friends, for this activity try to think of a person that others might be familiar with, too. Find a picture of this person and paste it in the space below. Find a quote by this person or a news article that depicts the person's values you admire and include it with the picture.

Processing: Celebrity Role Model

What is it about this person that you admire?

_____

_____

_____

_____

_____

_____

In what ways are you similar to this person?

_____

_____

_____

_____

_____

_____

In what ways did you exhibit a quality similar to your role model this week?

In what ways do you hope to be more similar to this person?

_____

_____

_____

_____

_____

_____

If this person were a counselor, how might he or she interact with clients, be a leader in the field, and demonstrate counselor professional identity?

_____

_____

_____

_____

_____

_____

What aspects of yourself are you particularly proud of, or think might pair well with your role model? What traits do you possess that you could share with or pass on to your role model?

_____

_____

_____

_____

_____

_____

Taking It to the Group

- Provide feedback to group members on ways they already might be similar to the role models they selected.

- In what ways might the group support members to strive for the qualities that were valued in their role models?

- Who are some counseling role models that the group collectively admire? What is it about these people that is admirable?

- What is useful about having role models or seeking qualities that keep challenging us to continue striving and evolving?

- Discuss how the shared counseling professional philosophy may have been built on striving for particular values, perspectives, or to meet specific challenges.

My additional thoughts and feelings about the
Celebrity Role Model **activity...**

Supervisor Reflections

Follow-up Supervision Group Activities

- How can you be each other's role models? Identify ways in which members of the group act as role models to one another. Take time to share this information and let group members know how they influence the rest of the group in positive ways.

- Create a group scrapbook of counselor role models who demonstrate strong professional identities. Include quotes, stories, and noteworthy article abstracts if possible.

- Have a "dress up party" where everyone pretends to be their role models for part of the group meeting. Allow time for members to interact with one another while playing their part.

Activity 27: ABCs & 123s

Directions: Identify a value you hold for each letter of the alphabet (e.g., A is for altruism). Then, rank each value from most important to you (1) to least important (26). These values may be a combination of both professional and personal.

A_CB_s & 1₃2_s

A _____

B _____

C _____

D _____

E _____

F _____

G _____

H _____

I _____

J _____

K _____

L _____

M _____

N _____

1. _____

2. _____

3. _____

4. _____

5. _____

6. _____

7. _____

8. _____

9. _____

10. _____

11. _____

12. _____

13. _____

14. _____

O _____

P _____

Q _____

R _____

S _____

T _____

U _____

V _____

W _____

X _____

Y _____

Z _____

15. _____

16. _____

17. _____

18. _____

19. _____

20. _____

21. _____

22. _____

23. _____

24. _____

25. _____

26. _____

Processing: ABCs & 123s

How was the process of identifying a value for each letter of the alphabet? Did you get stuck?

_____

_____

_____

_____

_____

_____

When you review your list of values, are there more that reflect your professional beliefs or your personal beliefs? How do your personal beliefs inform your professional ones?

_____

_____

_____

_____

_____

_____

Discuss one value that you acted upon this week.

What values are identified in your top five? Discuss how you determined their rank order.

_____

_____

_____

_____

_____

_____

What values are identified in your bottom five? Discuss how you determined their rank order.

_____

_____

_____

_____

_____

_____

In what ways are your values evident to your co-workers, professors, supervisors, and clients?

_____

_____

_____

_____

_____

_____

Taking It to the Group

- We each hold similar and different values. Have group members share their top five and put this on a whiteboard to determine the group consensus. Allow each group member to discuss these further.

- Are there values some group members included on their list that other group members did not include? Spend time understanding the impact these values have on their professional identities.

- Discuss ways members can respond ethically when values are confronted by clients.

- What is some advice that the group might offer to an incoming practicum or internship group regarding core values and their relationship with professional identity development?

- What are ways the group can advocate for a client that represents the opposite of your values?

My additional thoughts and feelings about the *ABCs & 123s activity...*

Supervisor Reflections

Follow-up Supervision Group Activities

- As group members share their values, what emotions are evoked for other members? What reactions are group members experiencing? Allow time to respond to each other. Spend time examining these responses.

- As a group, spend time creating your values for your supervision group. Consider what expectations you have for each other and the group.

- As a group, review the alphabet and identify values that have not been shared for each letter. Ask group members to respond to these values. Are there any that fit with group members or with professional counseling?

Activity 28: Parts Picnic

Directions: It's time for a picnic. All of your parts (the many personalities, qualities, or traits within you) are getting together. Each of the parts has a different name, different goal, and hold different values. We know we can change in different environments we are in and hold different focuses depending on the intention of our part. Create your parts below, giving each a name, goal, and values.

PART 1	PART 2	PART 3
Name _____	Name _____	Name _____
Goal _____	Goal _____	Goal _____
Values _____	Values _____	Values _____
PART 4	**PART 5**	**PART 6**
Name _____	Name _____	Name _____
Goal _____	Goal _____	Goal _____
Values _____	Values _____	Values _____

Processing: Parts Picnic

How did you begin identifying your parts?

_____

_____

_____

_____

_____

_____

How many parts do you have? How do they interact together within you?

_____

_____

_____

_____

_____

_____

Which part(s) of you came out this week?

Reflecting on the values you identified for each part, are there any conflicts?

_____

_____

_____

_____

_____

_____

When are times that your "parts" interact with one another? Explain. (E.g., your sense of humor interacting with your fun side).

_____

_____

_____

_____

_____

_____

When are times that your parts interfere with one another or conflict? How do you manage your parts in those times? (E.g., your fun side or your sense of humor interacting with your sense of hard work or professionalism).

_____

_____

_____

_____

_____

_____

Taking It to the Group

- As a group, share the parts you would like the group to know. What are the similarities and differences among our parts in the group?

- Reflecting on the values each part holds, specifically those that are contradictory, how do we address the differences?

- Can we identify instances where our values interfered with our work or conflicted with our counseling ethical codes? How do we resolve these conflicts?

- Understanding our parts is important to your professional identity. Have group members discuss ways that their parts inform their professional identities.

- How can we advocate for our clients examining their parts? What ways can we support our client's journey to understanding themselves?

My additional thoughts and feelings about the
Parts Picnic **activity...**

Supervisor Reflections

Follow-up Supervision Group Activities

- It's time for the parts to party together! Following Satir's (1978) model and Carlock (2015), have group members select one part of themselves and role-play a party. Rotate through the different parts.

- As a group, examine if there are parts of one another that could be detrimental to future clients.

- Spend time having group members modify any of their parts they either omitted intentionally or became more aware of through the group supervision conversation.

References

American Counseling Association. (2014). *Code of ethics*. Retrieved from www.counseling.org/resources/aca-code-of-ethics.pdf

Bloom, Z. D., McNeil, V. A., Flasch, P., & Sanders, F. (2018). A comparison of empathy and sympathy between counselors-in-training and their non-counseling academic peers. *Professional Counselor, 8*(4), 341–354. doi:10.15241/zdb.8.4.341

Bridges, J. G., Hicks, A., Lazzo, P., & Keegan, S. (2019). Navigating the moral realm of counseling: Counselor's expressed role within and awareness of value conversion. *The Family Journal: Counseling and Therapy for Couples and Families, 27*(2), 1–11. doi:10.1177/1066480719832505

Carlock, C. J. (2015). The solo parts party. *Satir International Journal, 3*(1), 36–57.

Corey, G., Corey, M. S., Corey, C., & Callanan, P. (2015). *Issues and ethics in the helping professions* (9th ed.). Stamford, CT: Cengage Learning.

Cottone, R. R., & Tarvydas, V. (2016). *Ethics and decision making in counseling and psychotherapy* (4th ed.). New York, NY: Springer.

Council for Accreditation of Counseling and Related Educational Programs. (2016). *CACREP accreditation standards and procedures manual*. Alexandria, VA: Author.

Crethar, H. C., & Winterowd, C. L. (2012). Values and social justice in counseling. *Counseling and Values, 57*(1), 3–9. doi:10.1002/j.2161-007X.2012.00001.x

Dollarhide, C. T. (2013). Using a values-based taxonomy in counselor education. *Counseling and Values, 58*(2), 221–236. doi:10.1002/j.2161-007X.2013.00035.x

Gibson, D. M., Dollarhide, C. T., & Moss, J. M. (2010). Professional identity development: A grounded theory of transformational tasks of new counselors. *Counselor Education and Supervision, 50*(1), 21–38. doi:10.1002/j.1556-6978.2010.tb00106.x

Levitt, D. H., & Aligo, A. A. (2013). Moral orientation as a component of ethical decision making. *Counseling and Values, 58*(2), 195–204. doi:10.1002/j.2161-007X.2013.00033.x

Lloyd-Hazlett, J., & Foster, V. A. (2017). Student counselors' moral, intellectual, and professional ethical identity development. *Counseling and Values, 62*(1), 90–105. doi:10.1002/crj.12051

Moorhead, H. J. H., Gill, C., Minton, C. A. B., & Myers, J. E. (2012). Forgive and forget? Forgiveness, personality, and wellness among counselors-in-training. *Counseling and Values, 57*(1), 81–95. doi:10.1002/j.2161-007X.2012.00010.x

Moss, J. M., Gibson, D. M., & Dollarhide, C. T. (2014). Professional identity development: A grounded theory of transformational tasks of counselors. *Journal of Counseling & Development, 92*(1), 3–12. doi:10.1002/j.1556-6676.2014.00124.x

Satir, V. (1978). *Your many faces*. Mountain View, CA: Celestial Arts.

Young, A., Dollarhide, C. T., & Baughman, A. (2015). The voices of school counselors: Essential characteristics of school counselor leaders. *Professional School Counseling, 19*(1), 36–45. doi:10.5330/2156759X1501900101

CHAPTER 8

BUILDING COMMUNITY THROUGH CREDENTIALS AND PROFESSIONAL ORGANIZATIONS

Counselor professional identity includes being trained specifically in counselor education in preparation to hold related licenses and certifications, as well as interacting with others in the field through professional activities and organizations (Woo & Henfield, 2015; Woo, Storlie, & Baltrinic, 2016). Spurgeon (2012) highlighted these two counseling professional identity components by stressing the importance of building community relationships through opportunities provided in specialized training from counselor educators, Council for Accreditation of Counseling and Related Educational Programs (CACREP) common curriculum, and participation in counseling organizations such as the American Counseling Association (ACA). Burns and Cruikshanks (2018) provided evidence of this claim when they determined that independently licensed counselors, when reflecting on their professional identity, placed value in being trained in CACREP programs with counselor educators who held professional memberships, licenses, and certifications.

Having contact with counselors who hold a strong professional identity is essential in building one's own identity as a counselor and becoming indoctrinated in the field (Luke & Goodrich, 2010). For professional counselors, this exposure to the field begins with training. CACREP (2016) standards indicate that accredited counselor education programs must have at least three full-time core faculty members who hold doctorates in counselor education and maintain licensure and certifications, as well as membership in professional organizations (Section 1.W; Section 1.X). This underscores the importance of counselor trainees being introduced to the field and trained by faculty members with strong professional identities. Counselor educators are trained specifically to teach counseling content and skills to students who aspire to be counselors. Through their doctoral training, they learn advanced counseling skills and content, as well as teaching and research methods to prepare them to train counselors and further the empirical inquiries in the field. Counselor educators are often leaders in the field via their research but also by holding leadership positions in counseling organizations and presenting at professionals conferences. Being mentored by counselor educators as they demonstrate strong professional identity is a unique and important part of counselor trainee experience.

Counselor trainees also have shared training standards specific to counseling that prepares them for licensure and certification. CACREP is an important organization in the counseling field as it ensures that professional counselors have common training and curriculum experiences (Spurgeon, 2012). Upon graduating from a CACREP accredited counseling program, students are often prepared for licensure and certification requirements. Licensure is important for counselor professionals as it ensures counselors practice within their expertise and therefore protect the public from harm (Spurgeon, 2012). Questions on the National Counselor Exam for Licensure and Certification (NCE), which is the required exam for many state license processes, as well as being endorsed as a National Certified Counselor (NCC), are built upon CACREP's eight content areas (National Board of Certified Counselors, 2016–2017). Though, currently, there is no federal counseling license or portability between states, CACREP provides a metric to ensure that counselors trained across the country have knowledge and experience with the same educations standards and content (Mascari & Webber, 2013). In the year 2022, the NCC credential will be restricted to graduates from CACREP programs (American Counseling Association, 2014), which further endorses the importance of having this standardized counseling curriculum.

Membership and involvement in professional organizations is another important aspect of counselor professional identity. When counselors join organizations on the national, regional, or state level, they are part of a community of counselors with shared training, license or certification, work, and vision. Professional organizations not only promote the profession through advocacy efforts, but also provide members with resources, opportunities, and a sense of community. Organizations such as the American Counseling Association (ACA) and Chi Sigma Iota (CSI) have missions aimed at enhancing professional identity and advancing the counseling field. The American School Counselor Association (ASCA) and the American Mental Health Counselors Association (AMHCA) promote and advocate for school counselors and mental health counselors, respectively. Leaders in all of these organizations are working "behind-the-scenes" to improve the competence and advancement of the counseling field. For example, ACA, ASCA, and AHMCA have their own respective codes of ethics used to ensure their constituents have ethical guidelines and each work to improve legislation to ensure the work of professional counselors can have a more expansive reach to the public.

The American Counseling Association is arguably the largest organization that works to improve the professional identity of counselors. The ACA has various divisions focused on specialized interest areas (e.g., assessment and research, creativity in counseling, social justice) or populations and areas of practice (e.g., adult development and aging, child and adolescent, college counseling, and multicultural counseling and development). Regional groups and branches that represent local constituents of ACA on a regional or state level, as well as territories and international locations, are also included under ACA. Local and state branches are useful, as they have the opportunity to focus on the unique needs of counselors within the state and provide statewide advocacy and competency efforts (Darcy & Abed-Faghri, 2013). Chi Sigma Iota (CSI), the international counseling academic and professional honor society, is another influential organization for professional counselors. Chi Sigma Iota promotes excellence and leadership in counseling and has hundreds of chapters. Involvement in CSI promotes professional identity and provides many leadership opportunities, which ultimately lead to enhanced professional connections and participation in other professional organizations (Luke & Goodrich, 2010). Unlike other professional organizations, in order to have membership in CSI one must be enrolled in or have obtained a degree in a counselor education program. Further, CSI only allows active chapters to be in CACREP accredited programs (Chi Sigma Iota, 2018).

There are many advantages to being an active member of professional organizations. Members might have access to journals, newsletters, and other resources, as well as continuing education and annual conferences. At conferences, professional counselors can obtain continuing education required for license and certification renewals and be surrounded and engaged by peers. There are opportunities to stay current in events and professional advances, as well as seek consultation and refresh skills and counseling content. Involvement in the activities of professional organizations and staying connected to others in the field can offer a sense of belonging (Shillingford, Trice-Black, & Butler, 2013; Woo et al., 2016). When counselors attend conferences they can leave feeling reconnected to the profession and refreshed; ready to get back to their daily work responsibilities.

When counselors demonstrate professional identity by holding licenses and certifications, as well as maintaining involvement in professional organizations, they are able to be part of a larger group of professionals. This larger community provides a united front to the public and represents professional counseling. Licensure and certification provide evidence that professional counselors have completed the necessary education and standards of knowledge to practice. Having an active membership with professional organizations can provide a shared sense of belonging as a counselor. Membership alone, though, is not a measure of professional identity (Cashwell, Kleist, & Scofield, 2009). In organizations like ACA,

ASCA, and AMHCA members are not required to have a master's or doctoral degree in counselor education. Therefore, Cashwell et al. (2009) indicated professional identity is a culmination of membership, education, licensure and credentials, and service and leadership. As such, counselor trainees and professional counselors should consider the impact of building a professional community and remaining connected to the counseling discipline through a variety of ways.

Connecting Credentials and Professional Organizations to You

The activities within this chapter are aimed at helping you consider your own belonging within the professional community of counselors. You are asked to consider what license and credentials you might eventually need or want and begin researching the requirements in obtaining them. This will be useful for you as you start to gather material for the license and credentialing process, as well as to inform you on what might lie ahead in terms of post-graduate workshops or experiences. Though requirements sometimes change, it will be good to have all of this information and related resources in one place as you prepare for your professional future.

You are also invited to research the various divisions of ACA to find one that meets your interests and that can help you build a sense of community and belonging in the profession. Through your investigation, you will be asked to consider all of the advantages and benefits for being part of the organization and summarize it on an advertisement billboard. Sometimes, we can forget all of the opportunities and resources provided by professional organizations. Some "selling points" for ACA divisions might include a journal or newsletter with topics specific to the division interest area, conferences where like-minded counselors meet to present and discuss relevant topics, grants to promote research and service related to its mission, and continuing education offerings available complimentary to members.

We will also ask you to take your explorations even further by encouraging you to create a vision board where you can lay out your professional dreams and aspirations related to professional identity. This is an opportunity to consider how you can spend your time and offer your strengths to the profession. You might consider your own leadership roles or ways to advocate for the advancement of counseling. Finally, professional organizations take an important role in advocating for professional counseling. As such, you are asked to consider your own role in professional advocacy by formulating a letter or phone call with the purpose of speaking on behalf of, and promoting, professional counseling.

Activity 29: Credentials: Alphabet Soup after Your Name

Directions: Licensure and credentials are important to regulate the counseling field and protect the public. They exist to ensure counselors meet educational and clinical requirements mandated by the body issuing the license. Consider your professional goals and the license and/or credentials required to do entry-level work (e.g., state counseling license or school counseling credential). Looking ahead to the future, think about other credentials you want to enhance your work or meet vocational aspirations (e.g., supervision endorsement, credential in a specific technique or for a presenting problem or population). For this activity, do some research into the license and/or credentials you intend to obtain. Create a to-do list of the necessary steps and requirements below. Consider listing resources or websites so that you have this document as a resource for the future.

License or Credential: _____

☐ _____

☐ _____

☐ _____

☐ _____

☐ _____

License or Credential: _____

☐ _____

☐ _____

☐ _____

☐ _____

☐ _____

License or Credential: _____

☐ _____

☐ _____

☐ _____

☐ _____

☐ _____

License or Credential: _____

☐ _____

☐ _____

☐ _____

☐ _____

☐ _____

Processing: Credentials: Alphabet Soup after Your Name

What steps have you already taken to do preliminary work toward these licensure or credentialing goals?

_____

_____

_____

_____

_____

_____

What educational components do you have that will help you meet these goals? Be specific and list coursework and/or specific CACREP standards that will help you meet requirements.

_____

_____

_____

_____

_____

_____

_____

When were times this week you were reminded of the importance
of counselor licensure and/or credentialing?

List people you know who have these licensures and/or credentials. Write down some questions about the process they can answer to help inform you better as you embark on a similar journey.

_____

_____

_____

_____

_____

_____

If you do not know people with these credentials, what might you do to learn more about the process in obtaining them?

_____

_____

_____

_____

_____

_____

When will you need to look back at this list? When will you be ready to seek some of these credentials?

_____

_____

_____

_____

_____

_____

Taking It to the Group

- Share the information learned among the group and take time for members to add steps or resources they may have missed.

- How can the group be supportive to one another in obtaining these professional goals of licensure and credentialing?

- What do members need from the group leader, or supervisor, in order to gain more information from someone seasoned in this licensure or credentialing process? What do members need from other more advanced counselors that are available to them?

- What are some resources that the group can share with others who have similar goals? Consider making a resource list for future interns in their program or at the counseling sites.

- Overall, how do licensure and credentialing processes promote counseling professional identity?

My additional thoughts and feelings about the
Credentials: Alphabet Soup after Your Name **activity...**

Supervisor Reflections

Follow-up Supervision Group Activities

- How does the group feel about license portability? Discuss the possible benefits and challenges of license portability.

- Investigate the licensure and/or credentialing boards in your state. Brainstorm questions to email the board in order to learn more about its members' work and responsibilities as state leaders.

- If possible, attend an open meeting of your state's licensure board. Alternatively, obtain meeting minutes from a past meeting to review during group time.

Activity 30: Billboard Advertisement

Directions: Membership in The American Counseling Association and its many divisions is an important part of counseling professional identity. Participation in the association can provide counselors with a sense of belonging and community with others who have common professional interests and strengths, counseling resources, and offer leadership opportunities. For this activity, research the American Counseling Association divisions and choose one of interest to learn more about. With the information you gather about the division, create a billboard in the space below to advertise it to other counselors.

Processing: Billboard Advertisement

What factors lead you to choose this ACA division to advertise?

_____

_____

_____

_____

_____

_____

How can this ACA division, or any other one, enhance your professional identity?

_____

_____

_____

_____

_____

_____

Who do you know that has membership with the ACA divisions you researched?

ACA, its divisions, and other professional organizations often do "behind-the-scenes" work to promote the profession and support counselors and the general public. What kind of work does this division do to serve that mission?

_____

_____

_____

_____

_____

What strengths do you have that would help you be able to contribute to this division?

_____

_____

_____

_____

_____

_____

Flash forward five years in the future. How do you see your involvement with this division evolve over time?

_____

_____

_____

_____

_____

_____

Taking It to the Group

- Take turns sharing the information each member learned about ACA divisions. Provide feedback to group members regarding the divisions they chose to advertise (e.g., in what ways did members choose groups that fit their interests and strengths?).

- As a group, use some time together to extend learning to divisions that were not selected by group members.

- Considering the group's specific state and community, what ACA division is particularly important and why? If the group were to create a new division that meets the specific needs of the group's community, what would it be?

- What steps can the group do to provide more information about ACA and its division to other supervisees or counselors in your program or at your counseling sites?

- What is the role that ACA, its divisions, and other professional organizations have in promoting and advocating for professional counseling?

My additional thoughts and feelings about the
***Billboard Advertisement* activity...**

Supervisor Reflections

Follow-up Supervision Group Activities

- If the group created a new division that met the needs of the community, what would the mission of the division be and what resources to area counselors can it provide?

- Create a bulletin board in your department or counseling site to highlight and demonstrate select divisions and provide others with information regarding their resources and missions.

- Take turns bringing in division newsletters at each group meeting to review and keep up on current events within the field or the division.

Activity 31: Vision Board

Directions: A vision board can keep us focused on our plan for the future. It is a space to summarize goals and objectives, as well as the driving forces that underlie work. Vision boards can be made up of different words, pictures of people or their names, illustrations, motivational quotes, aspirations, and anything else that keeps us on our professional path. As with all forward movement and progress, there might be bumps in the road, distractions, or alternate routes in the achievement of our goals. A vision board can keep the end goal in mind and remind us of those underlying hopes and dreams.

On the next page is a vision board for you to decorate. Think about your professional goals and the motivating factors you have to achieve them. Reflect on your hopes and dreams and envision an ideal professional future. Think about the different populations you could impact and work with as a professional counselor, including the various roles you might take over the years. Consider the below organizations, as well as the licenses and specialty certifications you can obtain, to help you achieve your goals. Feel free to glue items to your board (magazine clippings, newspapers, photographs, printed items, etc.). You may also use pictures, drawings, words, and/or affirmations to create what you want your board to look like.

Organizations to Consider

- American Counseling Association
- Association for Counselor Education & Supervision
- American School Counselor Association
- Association for Adult Development and Aging
- Association for Assessment and Research in Counseling
- Association for Child and Adolescent Counseling
- Association for Creativity in Counseling
- American College Counseling Association
- Association for Humanistic Counseling
- Association for Lesbian, Gay, Bisexual and Transgender Issues in Counseling
- Association for Multicultural Counseling and Development
- American Mental Health Counselors Association
- American Rehabilitation Counseling Association
- Association for Spiritual, Ethical, and Religious Values in Counseling
- Association for Specialists in Group Work
- Counselors for Social Justice
- International Association of Addictions and Offender Counselors
- International Association of Marriage and Family Counselors
- Military and Government Counseling Association
- National Career Development Association
- National Employment Counseling Association
- Association for Play Therapy

License/Certifications

Certified School Counselor	Licensed Professional Counselor
National Certified Counselor	National Certified Mental Health Counselor
Registered Play Therapist	National Certified School Counselor
Approved Clinical Supervisor	Certified Addictions Specialist

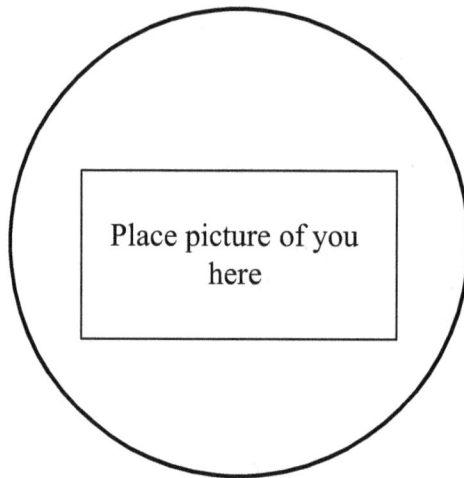

Place picture of you
here

Processing: Vision Board

How did you create your vision board? Describe the process.

_____

_____

_____

_____

_____

_____

Who or what is included in your vision board? How do these people or factors represent a driving force for you to achieve your professional dreams?

_____

_____

_____

_____

_____

_____

Where have you experienced your visions this week?

If you could describe your vision board in ten words of fewer, what would it say?

_____

_____

_____

_____

_____

_____

Did you learn anything new about where you want to go on your professional journey?

_____

_____

_____

_____

_____

_____

_____

In what ways does your vision board capture your motivations for becoming a professional counselor and achieving your professional dreams?

_____

_____

_____

_____

_____

_____

Taking It to the Group

- Allow each group member to share their vision board. Spend time discussing each one, asking questions, and learning more about the group's professional visions.

- What themes emerged for the group? Do group members still need more understanding and support to accomplish their vision boards? Are group members clear or unsure of their professional path?

- How does the group think that envisioning futures and achieving professional goals is related to counselor professional identity?

- What are some ways that peer supervision would be useful in supporting group members' vision boards?

- How does the group envision the future of professional counseling? What might be included in a professional counseling vision board?

**My additional thoughts and feelings about the
Vision Board activity...**

Supervisor Reflections

Follow-up Supervision Group Activities

- If the group space allows, have group members hang their vision boards. This can serve as a reminder of their professional journey.

- As a group, brainstorm some other ideas that could be included in future vision boards and how an exercise like this could be useful with future clients.

- Allow each group member the opportunity to share what their motivation was for entering the field of professional counseling. Is it still the same goal? Discuss how it has changed.

Activity 32: Advocating for Counseling

Directions: Advocacy is an important topic in professional counseling and one that all counselors support. Advocacy can be used in many ways. At times, we advocate individually for our clients or we advocate for their relationships and other environments which impact them. There are times we need to advocate for our profession on a larger scale. There are times when decisions are made from elected officials or other businesses which have a greater impact on our clients. We also know some of our clients are not able to advocate for themselves. As a profession, we support our clients and the counseling field.

Think about an underserved population that needs more services and support. Research who you would need to contact in order to obtain more services for this group (i.e., Local Government Workers, State Legislators, Federal Officials). Alternatively, you can also advocate for a professional counseling cause. Create a brief script you would use in your phone call, email, or meeting with the official. This should be from the counselor perspective and focus on the population or cause. Consider what the population needs and the potential impact more services would provide, or how the public would benefit from the identified cause related to professional counseling.

Remember, your time will be limited so you need to be concise and direct with your message.

Processing: Advocating for Counseling

What population did you select or what professional issue did you advocate for? What drew you to that population or cause?

_____

_____

_____

_____

_____

_____

How would that population benefit from advocacy? Or, how would the profession or general public benefit from advocacy for the professional issue you may have identified?

_____

_____

_____

_____

_____

_____

How did you use advocacy skills this week?

How did you create your message? Who do you need to work with in order to advocate for this population/ professional issue?

_____

_____

_____

_____

_____

_____

What strengths do you have that help you be an effective advocate? What does advocacy require? What strengths do you have that help you be an effective advocate?

_____

_____

_____

_____

_____

_____

What do you think the impact of advocacy has on the profession? How does advocating for clients, specifically those who are underserved, and professional issues reflect the definition and philosophy of counseling?

_____

_____

_____

_____

_____

_____

Taking It to the Group

- Discuss the process of creating a script to demonstrate how to advocate. How do you deliver your message when legislators receive numerous calls about numerous populations?

- Though group members may have advocated for different populations or causes, what were some shared messages amongst the group? How did these similarities reflect counselor professional identity?

- As a group, spend time understanding what the role government and business officials have in making decisions for our clients? Share past instances where the counseling field has used their education, knowledge, and strong membership to impact harmful decisions these entities may make.

- What is some advice that the group might offer to an incoming practicum or internship group regarding your responsibility as an advocate within the development of your professional counselor identity?

- How can we advocate on a smaller scale for our clients, as well as the profession?

My additional thoughts and feelings about the
Advocating for Counseling **activity...**

Supervisor Reflection

Follow-up Supervision Group Activities

- If the group space allows, have group members select a population and follow through on the advocacy plan. Have students make phone calls, send emails, and hold meetings (as appropriate) to fully experience the commitment that the counseling field has to advocacy.

- As a group, list some other ideas that could be useful when incorporating advocacy into your practice as a professional counselor.

- Allow each group member the opportunity to share any experiences they have had with advocacy. What did they do specifically? What did they learn in this process for future advocacy work?

References

American Counseling Association. (2014). *NCC status will require graduation from a CACREP accredited program beginning in 2022*. Retrieved from www.counseling.org/news/updates/2014/11/19/ncc-status-will-require-graduation-from-a-cacrep-accredited-program-beginning-in-2022

Burns, S. T., & Cruikshanks, D. R. (2018). Independently licensed counselors' connection to CACREP and state professional identity requirements. *The Professional Counseling, 8*(10), 29–45. doi:10.15241/stb.8.1.29

Cashwell, C. S., Kleist, D., & Scofield, T. (2009). A call for professional unity. *Counseling Today, 52*(2), 60–61.

Chi Sigma Iota. (2018). *Chapter FAQ*. Retrieved from www.csi-net.org/page/Chapter_FAQ

Council for Accreditation of Counseling and Related Educational Programs. (2016). *CACREP accreditation standards and procedures manual*. Alexandria, VA: Author.

Darcy, M. G., & Abed-Faghri, N. M. (2013). The relationship between counselors and their state professional association: Exploring counselor professional identity. *Professional Counselor, 3*(3), 152–160. doi:10.15241/mgd.3.3.152

Luke, M., & Goodrich, K. M. (2010). Chi Sigma Iota chapter leadership and professional identity development in early career counselors. *Counselor Education and Supervision, 50*(1), 56–78. doi:10.1002/j.1556-6978.2010.tb00108.x

Mascari, J. B., & Webber, J. (2013). CACREP accreditation: A solution to license portability and counselor identity problems. *Journal of Counseling & Development, 91*, 15–25. doi:10.1002/j.1556-6676.2013.00066.x

National Board for Certified Counselors. (2016–2017). *Candidate Handbook for national certification with the national counselor examination for licensure and certification (NCS)*. Greensboro, NC: Author. Retrieved from https://nbcc.org/Assets/Exam/Handbooks/NCE.pdf

Shillingford, M. A., Trice-Black, S., & Butler, S. K. (2013). Wellness of minority counselor educators. *Counselor Education and Supervision, 52*, 255–269. doi:10.1002/j.1556-6978.2013.00041.x

Spurgeon, S. L. (2012). Counselor identity: A national imperative. *Journal of Professional Counseling: Practice, Theory, & Research, 39*, 3–16. doi:10.1080/15566382.2012.12033878

Woo, H., & Henfield, M. S. (2015). Professional identity scale in counseling (PISC): Instrument development and validation. *Journal of Counselor Leadership and Advocacy, 2*, 93–112. doi:10.1080/2326716X.2015.1040557

Woo, H., Storlie, C., & Baltrinic, E. R. (2016). Perceptions of professional identity development from counselor educators in leadership positions. *Counselor Education and Supervision, 55*, 278–293. doi:10.1002/ceas.12054

CHAPTER 9

CAREER EXPLORATION

Career identity has changed throughout the past years with a different focus. It is no longer "linear and hierarchical, but multifaceted, unstable, cyclical, and transitional over the life course" (Bimrose & Hearne, 2012, p. 338). There is a focus on identifying areas of strength, interest, values, personality, experiences, ability, and other life events that contribute to your own personal development which blends with your career interaction, focusing on the interaction of work, and life roles (CACREP, 2016).

The process of career exploration and career counseling has evolved in professional counseling. There is a greater emphasis on integrating both professional goals with personal lifestyle goals. Based on this ever-changing field (Bimrose & Hearne, 2012), it brings to light the value of meaningful work as an important element in career counseling (Allan, Owens, & Duffy, 2017). This is highlighted by Council for Accreditation of Counseling and Related Educational Programs (CACREP) standards (2016) stressing the importance of incorporating the search for meaningful work into our counseling with clients. In order to move in this direction, it is necessary counselor trainees complete their own exploration and understand their views of their career path. Additionally, research has shown support for counselor trainees completing courses aimed at career counseling with an emphasis on theoretical integration in their own work, which is then translated into work with clients (Allan et al., 2017; Bimrose et al., 2018; Blount, Bjornsen, & Moore, 2018). This has been useful as the counseling field has continued to evolve over time. Counselors who specialize in career counseling found that the field changed and needed additional engagement to meet clients' needs. Neary (2014) found that career counselors reentering the field required postgraduate professional development to reconnect with changes in the field. The additional training led to empowerment of counselors and increasing their confidence to face the changing definition of career counseling. As such, it has been noted that the ability to address a client holistically still is valued in career counseling. This has been valuable in promoting sustainable change for clients to address their needs on a personal level, which then helped to address career needs (Maree & Di Fabio, 2018).

Marbley et al. (2015) examined moments that led professional counselors into the counseling field and factors that supported their reengagement with the profession. They found that life experiences influenced professional identity and career development for many counselors, which then impacted their career decisions. Many counselors highlighted their value of balance, support, helping, and honesty within their careers and recognized the need for these to prevent burnout and increase compassion satisfaction in their career (Blount et al., 2018). The risk of burnout remains high for professional counselors as the very nature of the counseling field makes counselors susceptible to stress and poor self-care (Wardle & Mayorga, 2016). Therefore, recognizing the signs of burnout and engaging in the profession with a strong professional identity is essential to remaining healthy for oneself and for clients. Engaging in intentional wellness is a strategy for both personal and professional maintenance, allowing for career sustainment.

The areas that counselor professionals have to address throughout their own career development varies from awareness of the personal impacts (Bimrose & Hearne, 2012), as well as incorporating the changing world and role of the counselor (Neary, 2014) and the demands placed on professional counselors.

Awareness of personal impacts recognizes the value of personal experiences, personal career timeline, personality, and workplace experiences. The needs of clients change, which forces counselor professionals to respond accordingly. At times, counselors are called to leadership roles to support their own development as educators, but ultimately have a positive impact on the counseling field and clients (Woo, Storlie, & Baltrinic, 2016). Professional counselors take into consideration the comprehensive approach they need in order to work with clients, at times diverting from career related topics in sessions. The ability to be flexible and in-tune with client concerns is essential to the success as a professional counselor (Maree & Di Fabio, 2018).

Career counseling is part of the CACREP standards (2016, Section 2.F.4), that require counselor trainees to understand specific theories to work with clients and find their connection to a career path that meets their personal goals. There is emphasis on the work-life balance, and a recent shift in the patterns of their career path toward that balance (Bimrose & Hearne, 2012). The skills needed for this area are gained through counselor education academic programs that help counselor trainees learn theory, techniques, and interventions that will help support clients' journeys to their career choice. It is also helpful for counselor trainees to employ many of these skills in their own development. This exploration of self is essential to determine strengths, abilities, preferences, and interests to move into areas that provide success in the personal and professional world. It is also important for counselors to develop a clear professional identity statement that identifies who they are as a professional (Burns, 2017). Applying the ideas of an elevator speech to concisely describe one's professional self helps to concisely express the key components of professional identity (Simpson, 2016). These are skills that a counselor can then impart onto the client.

The field emphasizes the need for career counselors to help clients find their own place and path. There are multiple ways the professional and personal career path intersect. It is important to recognize that the paths are not always separate areas and often need to be dealt with together, as there are multiple impacts that result with each area. For example, if a client loses his or her job, there is not only a professional impact, but a personal impact and they cannot be dealt with in isolation as the effect is too great. The career counselor works to blend these areas together to help the client move to a place where they can reflect and address each area separately and together.

Connecting Career Exploration to You

The activities in this chapter reflect your personal journey towards becoming a professional counselor. The intention is to help you examine your motivation for entering into this field and the ways that this field provides you with the balance you desire. It is a personal exploration though acknowledging who you are as a person and what you want for yourself and clients. Through reflecting on what this field has provided and what you hope to offer to the field, it begins to merge personal and professional selves together to gain a higher level of career satisfaction. The realities of burnout, compassion fatigue, and vicarious trauma are a threat to professional counselors, therefore addressing these areas and helping to find ways to continue to reconnect to the field, provides a foundation to persist amidst professional challenges.

One activity is designed to help combat the days of stress to reconnect you to the field and your motivations. Activities also support developing your speech to concisely express yourself and your commitment to the field in what you hope to accomplish (Burns, 2017; Simpson, 2016). The ability to reflect on who has impacted you as you entered into the counseling field, as well as messages and statements that empower you, help to shape you into the counselor you want to be. The lessons that have been learned along the way have kept you on this current path to becoming a professional counselor and will be important as you continue to move along in this journey. It is essential to take the time to reflect on your career path and how to continue to move yourself in the direction you choose.

Activity 33: Career Jar

Directions: There are times where we need a reminder of the impact we have on our clients or positive moments in our work. Sometimes we do not get to experience the outcome of our work with clients because of our limited time working together. There are also workdays that seem so hard and discouraging that we can't remember anything positive. Regardless, we do know the value and impact we might have on our clients, our work, and to the counseling field.

The purpose of this activity is to think about positive experiences in your work and moments where you feel reconnected to the reasons you wanted to be a counselor and proud of the work you are doing. Take a moment each day this week, and on the strips of paper on the next page write the positive experiences you had at your practicum or internship site. These can be accomplishments, success with a new technique, feedback from your site or university supervisor, or anything else. Don't skip a day, even if you have to dig deep for a positive experience. As you write these experiences, cut the papers and tape them into the jar (Figure 9.1) so you have them to remind you of your work. Alternatively, you can use a real jar and place the papers inside. Continue to write yourself daily or weekly messages. When there are times that you need a reminder as to why you entered this field of counseling or when you are feeling discouraged, your career jar will be full and ready to support you.

Figure 9.1 Career Jar
(Grmarc, 2019)

Processing: Career Jar

Describe the experience of taking a moment at the end of each day to identify your strengths and accomplishments while at your practicum and internship site.

_____

_____

_____

_____

_____

_____

What themes do you see emerging among what you identified?

_____

_____

_____

_____

_____

_____

What was your favorite moment that you experienced in practicum or internship this week?

You were directed to not skip a day of writing down positive experiences. Was there a day where you felt discouraged and like nothing positive happened? If so, discuss how you were still able to come up with something to list for your jar. If this did not happen, anticipate a time when it might be hard and how you will still be able to identify a strength even if it's small.

_____

_____

_____

_____

_____

_____

Did you have a day where you needed to go back into your jar for a reminder of your commitment to the field of counseling? Discuss why you needed to go into the jar and what it was like to get a reminder of the positives you previously wrote down? If you didn't need to go back into your jar, anticipate a time you might and describe that below.

_____

_____

_____

_____

_____

_____

How do you think this experience can assist in sustaining you career?

_____

_____

_____

_____

_____

_____

Taking It to the Group

- Have group members share content from the strips of paper they put in their career jars.

- Discuss any struggles group members had in identifying strengths or accomplishments. How might early career counselors struggle with finding accomplishments and strengths? Spend time providing each other additional feedback and help to consider areas they may have neglected when identifying positive experiences.

- Spend time sharing the difficulties that the field of counseling can pose to counselors, especially new counselors. Discuss potential self-care strategies that would be beneficial to support everyone's motivation to remain in the field.

- What is some advice that the group might offer to an incoming practicum or internship group regarding commitment to the field and the potential areas of burnout in the career of professional counseling?

- Consider some leaders in the professional counseling field. What are some victories or accomplishments these leaders may have experienced for the greater good of the profession?

My additional thoughts and feelings about the
Career Jar **activity...**

Supervisor Reflections

Follow-up Supervision Group Activities

- Have group members discuss other self-care strategies and activities that they engage in. Spend time discussing ways that are beneficial, short-term and long-term.

- As a group, consider some other ways you could use this career jar as you continue your counseling professional journey.

- Allow each group member the opportunity to provide a note to one another's career jar. The use of feedback and reflective listening can be used to help model this experience.

Activity 34: Elevator Speech

Directions: You are on an elevator at the bottom floor. You will take the elevator to the top floor and it will take approximately 30 seconds. In 70 words, 30 seconds at a regular pace, create your elevator speech. This speech should reflect who you are as a counselor by revealing your professional abilities, identity, and goals to a potential employer. Remember to communicate who you are, what you are looking for, how you can benefit from the job, and how the employer will benefit from you. GO!

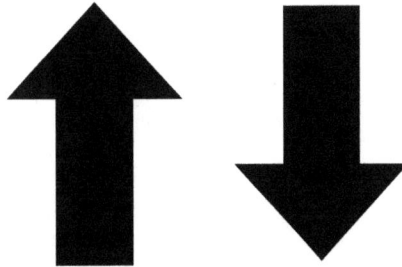

GOING UP

Processing: Elevator Speech

How did it feel to summarize yourself in 70 words and share it in 30 seconds?

_____

_____

_____

_____

_____

_____

What was most important for you to share with the potential employer?

_____

_____

_____

_____

_____

_____

Where have you experienced professional success this week?

In what ways were aspects of your counselor professional identity revealed in your speech?

_____

_____

_____

_____

_____

_____

Did your speech accomplish what you wanted? Was anything missing from your speech? What else would you share if you had more time and words?

_____

_____

_____

_____

_____

_____

How do you think this could be useful in future career experiences?

_____

_____

_____

_____

_____

_____

Taking It to the Group

- Allow each group member to share their elevator speech. Set a timer to see who is able to make their statement within 30 seconds, without altering their speech.

- Take turns giving each other feedback on how their professional identities were revealed in their speeches. If any group members experienced difficulty in summarizing their professional identity, abilities, and goals in a succinct way, provide some feedback and help.

- As a group, spend time reflecting on the value of learning how to speak concisely and succinctly. Where else in the field of counseling is this skill useful?

- What is some advice that the group might offer to an incoming practicum/internship group regarding communicating your professional identity in the field of professional counseling?

- What are some ways we can advocate for new opportunities for counselors in the workforce in ways that meet the definition and philosophy of counseling?

My additional thoughts and feelings about the
Elevator Speech **activity...**

Supervisor Reflections

Follow-up Supervision Group Activities

- Have group members discuss the struggle to speak concisely. Examine members' needs to say more, share more, and/or explain more. What is the value in less?

- As a group, identify five ways you can use the elevator speech when working with clients as an intervention.

- Read Burns (2017) and rewrite your speech following the recommended seven steps. Compare both speeches.

Activity 35: Supporting Roles

Directions: Everyone has voices of important people in their lives that influence them. For example, we might have one of our favorite professors giving us advice when we are working with a difficult client or we might remember a quote in a book about our favorite theory. For this activity, think about the people in your life whose "voices" are in your head in a positive and supportive way, or that you'd like to be in your head, when you are working. You might think of other counselors or counselor educators, or perhaps family members and friends who encourage you. There might be people who you have met, authors you have read, or speakers you have heard at conferences that you can include. Fill out the dialogue bubbles below and indicate the associated person by name, picture, or drawing.

Processing: Supporting Roles

Under what circumstances might some of these voices, sayings, or people be more pronounced or important to you?

_____

_____

_____

_____

_____

_____

If there are other counselors or counselor educators represented in your activity, how would you describe their professional identities and their influence over your own?

_____

_____

_____

_____

_____

_____

_____

When have you experienced appreciation for the supporting roles in your life this week?

How come some voices are louder, and stay with us longer, than others?

_____

_____

_____

_____

_____

_____

What are other influences to your counseling career? Aside from "voices," what are some influencing factors to how you counsel or how you demonstrate your professional identity (e.g., books, experiences)?

_____

_____

_____

_____

_____

_____

In what ways are you a "voice" to others? That is, what do other people see in you, or hear you saying, that might contribute to their "supporting roles?"

_____

_____

_____

_____

_____

_____

Taking It to the Group

- What are some common messages, themes, or people represented among the group?

- What were shared and unique experiences in how group members went about this activity and choosing the influential voices?

- Who are influential people and messages that influence how the supervision group operates with one another?

- How do other people, from our professional or personal lives, stay with us in our everyday functioning?

- Since community and connection to others is an important factor in counselor professional identity, how does identifying the individual people, messages, and voices that influence our work contribute to this sense of community and belonging?

My additional thoughts and feelings about the *Supporting Roles* activity...

Supervisor Reflections

Follow-up Supervision Group Activities

- Who has been influential to the group? Generate a list of people, quotes, or ideas that are influential to the supervision group.

- Create a group message, or motto, that group members can remember during their counseling session so that the group is always there for support.

- Give group members a piece of paper with their name on top and voice bubbles below. Circulate the papers around the group so that members can fill in the voice bubbles with sayings, ideas, or memories that they will remember about that person or the ways the person has been an inspiration. By the end of the activity, everyone will have a page filled with the ways they influence and contribute to their peers.

Activity 36: Current Issues and Breaking News

Directions: Staying up-to-date in the field is important for counselor professional identity. Think of hot topics, current issues, or news relevant to the categories below to complete the board for five in a row. Use blank spaces to explore something related to your own interests. List the topic below and add more information on the back if necessary.

CO	UN	SE	LI	NG
Newsletter Article	_____ _____	Technology	Quantitative Research	American Counseling Association
_____ _____	Conferences	Multicultural Counseling	Journal Article	Licensure Portability
Telemental Health	NBCC	Qualitative Research	A New Book Publication	_____ _____
Counseling Laws	Social Justice	_____ _____	CACREP	State/Local Counseling
ACA Division News	Professional Current Event	Innovative Technique	Counseling Laws	Ethics

CO	UN	SE	LI	NG

Processing: Current Issues and Breaking News

Pick one of the filled in squares to learn about more closely. Provide more information in the spaces provided.
Topic:

_____

_____

_____

_____

Who?

_____

_____

_____

_____

What?

_____

_____

_____

_____

When did hot topics or current events from the field become relevant to you this week?

Where?

_____

_____

_____

_____

When?

_____

_____

_____

_____

How?

_____

_____

_____

_____

Why?

_____

_____

_____

_____

Taking It to the Group

- Share your boards with one another, as well as the in-depth investigations of selected topics.

- What sources did everyone use in order to identity the current issues and news? How will the group remember the importance of these sources and continue to use them in the future?

- Make some plans to ensure the group stays aware of current events and keeps them in conversation during group supervision.

- What are some challenges in staying current on professional issues, and how can members work against these obstacles? What advice can the group offer to other counselors to promote being up-to-date on counseling news, topics, and literature?

- How is counseling professional identity dependent on counselors staying current on topics and issues relevant to the discipline?

My additional thoughts and feelings about the
Current Issues and Breaking News activity...

Supervisor Reflections

Follow-up Supervision Group Activities

- Create a new board that is made up of each group members' written-in responses from the original activity. As a group, discuss the squares and work to complete this new board.

- Draw a timeline of pivotal events in the history of counseling to learn more about the origins and development of the profession.

- Consider a current topic in counseling and brainstorm the multiple perspectives of that issue (e.g., pros and cons, viewpoints of different professional roles) and simulate a debate in which group members select "sides" to defend.

References

Allan, B. A., Owens, R. L., & Duffy, R. D. (2017). Generation me or meaning? Exploring meaningful work in college students and career counselors. *Journal of Career Development, 44*(6), 502–515. doi:10.1177/08945316667599

Bimrose, J., Brown, A., Mulvey, R., Kieslinger, B., Fabian, C. M., Schaefer, T., & Dewanti, R. T. (2018). Transforming identities and co-constructing careers of career counselors. *Journal of Vocational Behavior, 111*, 7–23. doi:10.1016/j.jvb.2018.07.008

Bimrose, J., & Hearne, L. (2012). Resilience and career adaptability: Qualitative studies of adult career counseling. *Journal of Vocational Behavior, 81*(3), 338–344. doi:10.1016/j.jvb.2012.08.002

Blount, A. J., Bjornsen, A. L., & Moore, M. M. (2018). Work values, occupational engagement, and professional quality of life in counselors-in-training: Assessments in a constructivist-based career counseling course. *Professional Counselor, 8*(1), 60–72.

Burns, S. T. (2017). Crafting a one-minute counselor professional identity statement. *Journal of Counselor Leadership and Advocacy, 4*(1), 66–76. doi:10.1080/2326716x.2017.1284623

Council for Accreditation of Counseling and Related Educational Programs. (2016). *CACREP accreditation standards and procedures manual.* Alexandria, VA: Author.

Grmarc. (2019). Isolated mason jar design [JPEG]. Retrieved from www.shutterstock.com/image-vector/isolated-mason-jar-design-517613755

Marbley, A. F., Bonner, F. A., II, Robinson, P. A., Stevens, H., Li, J., Phelan, K., & Huang, S. H. (2015). Voices from the field of social justice: Defining moments in our professional journeys. *Multicultural Education, 23*(1), 45–51.

Maree, J. G., & Di Fabio, A. (2018). Integrating personal and career counseling to promote sustainable development and change. *Sustainability, 10*(11), 2–16. doi:10.13390/su10114176

Neary, S. (2014). Reclaiming professional identity through postgraduate professional development: Career practitioners reclaiming their professional selves. *British Journal of Guidance & Counselling, 42*(2), 199–210. doi:10.1080/03069885.2013.869790

Simpson, D. (2016). "Going up?" A sport psychology consultant's guide to elevator speech. *Journal of Sport Psychology in Action, 7*(2), 109–120. doi:10.1080/21520704.2016.1182091

Wardle, E. A., & Mayorga, M. G. (2016). Burnout among the counseling profession: A survey of future professional counselors. *Journal of Educational Psychology, 10*(1), 9–15. doi:10.26634/jpsy.10.1.7068

Woo, H., Storlie, C. A., & Baltrinic, E. R. (2016). Perceptions of professional identity development from counselor educators in leadership positions. *Counselor Education and Supervision, 55*(4), 278–293. doi:10.1002/ceas.12054

CHAPTER 10

RESEARCH AND ASSESSMENT

Competency in assessment and research is a responsibility of counselors. Assessment is "the process of collecting in-depth information about a person in order to develop a comprehensive plan that will guide the collaborative counseling and service provision process" (ACA, 2014, p. 20). Assessment can be formal through standardized appraisal measures (e.g., inventories and tests) or informal via non-standardized methods (e.g., interviews and counselor-made questionnaires). Information gained from assessments can aid in diagnosis and treatment planning, conceptualization, evaluating suicidal ideation and other safety issues, decision-making, and tracking client progress. Research, as it relates to counseling, incudes knowing how to evaluate and analyze empirical studies as to glean evidenced-based practices for counseling (CACREP, 2016), as well as developing research competencies and use interventions grounded in theory or empirically based (ACA, 2014).

Assessment and testing, as well as research and program evaluation, are included in the CACREP (2016) standards, each representing its own common core domain. Assessment and testing (Section 2.F.7; CACREP, 2016) summarizes competencies including the history of its use in counseling, statistics and psychometric properties of assessments, using assessments for a variety of purposes and through various methods, and ethical and culture strategies when using and interpreting assessments. Research and program evaluation standards (CACREP, 2016, Section 2.F.8) indicate that accredited programs must include curriculum related to competencies such as evidenced-based practices, research design, development and evaluation of programs and interventions, data analysis, and ethical and cultural strategies for research and program evaluation.

Incorporating assessment and research to better inform the counseling process is a component of counselor professional identity. Watson (2012) suggested that the counseling profession values assessment in order to meet clients' unique needs more effectively. This includes a thorough cultural assessment that examines the intersectionality of clients' cultural variables and identities to inform counselors about the individuals they are counseling and avoid stereotyping (Ibrahim & Dykeman, 2011). The emphasis on learning about clients' unique experiences and phenomenological worldview reflects the idea that all clients should be seen as individuals with distinct characteristics regardless of their commonalities (e.g., presenting problem, age, gender, culture). Since counseling is built upon strengths, wellness, and empowerment, it is beneficial for counselors to use assessment practices to learn more about their clients and tailor treatment to clients' unique set of needs and distinct characteristics.

Providing evidenced-based treatment is also a vital aspect of counseling. Counselors are called to incorporate evidenced-based practices in their work in an effort to promote professional identity (Kaplan & Gladding, 2011). Choosing treatments and interventions that are empirically grounded upholds the integrity of the counseling discipline and wellbeing of clients (Hayden, 2017). When counselors provide treatment that has empirical support, it can legitimize their decision-making and therapeutic practice. This emphasizes not only the importance of being steeped in current literature but also having skills to understand the research.

As master's students in counseling will eventually work directly with clients, building their research competencies and associated research identity is pivotal (Jorgensen & Duncan, 2015). In their study of counselor trainees' research identity development, Jorgensen and Duncan (2015) found that though initially hesitant, participants linked their ultimate appreciation of research to their professional identity, as they wanted to be better counselors for their future clients. This indicated that counseling students gain awareness of the importance of building practice informed by research in order to be successful counselors. To do this, it is imperative for counselors to find available and current research, evaluate the methods used to discern its validity and transferability, and understand and apply implications from the research when appropriate. These are competencies included in CACREP (2016) standards and promoted in accredited counselor education programs.

Being adept at research is also essential for the successful use of formal assessments in counseling (Bardhoshi et al., 2016). Evaluating empirically grounded assessments and identifying ones that will be useful for the unique needs of each client is an essential skill and counselors can look to professional journals for evaluations of various assessments for a multitude of presenting problems (e.g., Bardhoshi et al., 2016; Erford, Jackson, Bardhoshi, Duncan, & Adalay, 2018). Counselors must be able to research and evaluate assessment tools and determine whether they are appropriate for their particular clientele. Counselors must be able to not only locate assessments, but also assess to ensure they are reliable and valid. Understanding norming procedures is also important in order to determine if results should be trusted without concern. For example, many assessments were normed on the White European-American population. Counselors working with clients of other races and cultures should assess the benefits and risks of using these assessments with their clients, as well as learn how to interpret and understand scores in the context of culture.

Not only is it important to understand how to interpret research as a way to promote evidenced-based practices, but having skills to develop and evaluate programs is also an essential proficiency for counselors. Opportunities to evaluate counseling programs can be integral to find ways to make improvements to and validate the work. Program evaluation is essential for the counseling profession so that counselors' work can be validated as effective and mental health services continue to be funded (Nielson, 2015). It also has the potential to verify professional counselor efforts or substantiate the philosophy and skill base of members of the profession. For example, Carey, Harrington, Martin, and Hoffman (2012) and Carey, Harrington, Martin, and Stevenson (2012) conducted statewide evaluations of Nebraska and Utah, respectively, high school counseling programs that followed the American School Counseling Association (ASCA) National Model to determine how the model correlated with positive student outcomes. Both studies provided evidence that the ASCA model was beneficial to students and therefore substantiated the ASCA model, as well as the work of school counselors.

In summary, competencies in assessment, testing, research, and program evaluation are important to promote the professional identity of counseling. Counselors proficient in these skills can assess client needs and their phenomenological perspectives more effectively in order to provide better service, discern evidenced-based practices to ensure interventions and skills are empirically grounded, and evaluate their own work and program outcomes to assess effectiveness and ensure funding. These factors aim to promote the definition and philosophical tenets of counseling (e.g., providing individualized treatment unique to clientele, use evidenced-based practices) and legitimize the work and roles of counselors via program evaluation.

Connecting Research and Assessment to You

In this chapter, activities are designed to help you consider the usefulness of assessment, research, and program evaluation, and to practice related skills when considering professional identity. You will be asked to delve into professional counseling research in an effort to sharpen your literature search skills and use them to find empirical studies that can be helpful to you as a developing counselor, as well as to potential clients.

For example, you will be asked to assess yourself and research self-identified areas for growth. Another activity will keep you connected to evidenced-based interventions by applying literature specifically to a fictional client.

Evaluating your career aspirations and skills in an effort to find goodness of fit with a professional position is another area of exploration. Here, you will apply program evaluation to your own abilities and interests in order to determine what kinds of work roles and environments might match you well. Follow up questions and group discussions related to these activities aim to help you consider how assessment, research, and evaluation skills are related to counselor professional identity. For example, using counseling resources and journals to help you find supporting literature and research or connecting the importance of thorough and multi-faceted assessment processes to ensure unique and individualized service to clientele. Considering aspects of assessment, research, and program evaluation as it relates to counseling can enhance the strength of your counselor professional identity and help you articulate its importance to professional counseling.

Activity 37: Research Your Needs

Directions: This workbook has activities that helped you focus on understanding yourself and areas you want to grow and change. Select one area of growth you have identified for yourself. Once you select this area, find three related research articles and synthesize the information from these articles. Specifically, examine ways the literature can directly inform an action plan to work on this area of growth. Then, create your action plan to support your growth as a professional counselor.

Area of Growth : _____

Article 1: _____

Article 2: _____

Article 3: _____

ACTION PLAN

Processing: Research Your Needs

How did you go about researching ideas related to your area of focus?

_____

_____

_____

_____

_____

_____

_____

What is the most important or interesting finding you came across regarding your area of growth?

_____

_____

_____

_____

_____

_____

_____

Where have you experienced the usefulness of research this week?

Processing: Research Your Needs

How did the articles support your movement towards growth in your identified area?

_____

_____

_____

_____

_____

_____

_____

As you created your action plan, based on research and evidence, how do you feel connected to the material?

_____

_____

_____

_____

_____

_____

_____

How will you use research in the future when examining yourself and your clients?

_____

_____

_____

_____

_____

_____

Taking It to the Group

- Allow time for each group member to share their areas for growth, as well as the related evidence-based information they researched. Discuss how the process of researching for personal use can be beneficial for professional practice.

- Reflect on the value of research and how it informs our professional work. How can we use research with our clients? Is there a time where research is not valued in our field? How can we add to the literature that exists to provide more knowledge and education?

- Discuss the process of synthesizing literature and connecting it to an action plan. Share ideas with each other on how to do this difficult process.

- What are some ways the group can continue to promote research in the field?

- Why is the role of research beneficial for counselor professional identity?

My additional thoughts and feelings about the
Research Your Needs **activity...**

Supervisor Reflections

Follow-up Supervision Group Activities

- Have group members bring in the articles they used to create the action plan. Share the articles among the group. Discuss any other findings.

- As a group, consider some of the action plans to address areas of growth. What are other considerations that may be useful? Is there other research that could be considered when looking to make changes?

- Discuss ways that this research could be used with program evaluation. How can research impact decisions made when implementing programs and determining effectiveness?

Activity 38: Case Study Reflection

Directions: As professional counselors, we use the concept of best practices to inform the direct work we do with our clients. Research helps to direct our goals, treatment plans, and interventions, as does our theoretical orientation. Consider the fictional case of Carlos (noted below). Then respond to each of the questions by completing more evidenced-based research.

CARLOS

Carlos is a 35-year-old Latino male who comes to counseling after experiencing depression that he believes is linked to being fired from two jobs within the last seven years and his inability to maintain romantic relationships.

On being fired from his jobs, he reported that both times his superiors gave the reason of "lack of performance." He reported that he had many "write-ups" before being fired for reasons such as: coming late to work, repeatedly calling in sick and missing important appointments, and not finishing assignments on time. He informs his counselor that often he was so nervous about particular job assignments or meetings that he would become physically sick. When he wasn't sick, he'd spend all night worrying about work, and "I'd just start drinking too much to calm myself down." Although he held extreme guilt over not doing "the best of my ability at work," he rationalized that it was better that he was not working "because I'm just not good enough at my job anyway. In fact, I'm not good at much."

Regarding his troubles with romantic relationships, Carlos explained, "Well, I'm 35, and I don't even have a girlfriend. By now I should be married with kids! What's wrong with me?" He shared that he has had girlfriends in the past, but "they always just break up with me." He reported that he thought he was going to marry his last girlfriend and asked her to move in, bought her gifts, and always wanted to spend time with her. He then reluctantly told you that they were only dating for three months. He reveals later that he had a long-term girlfriend in his late twenties to early thirties, who he broke up with just as things began to lead to talk of a commitment and possibly marriage.

When talking about his family of origin, he tells you that his father was an unhappy and angry man, who was often distant and rejecting. He says his mom is a wonderful woman who he wishes he lived closer to, "She was the best mother I could have asked for." You find out that Carlos is the oldest of three children, all boys. He gets along best with his youngest brother.

Apply your theory:

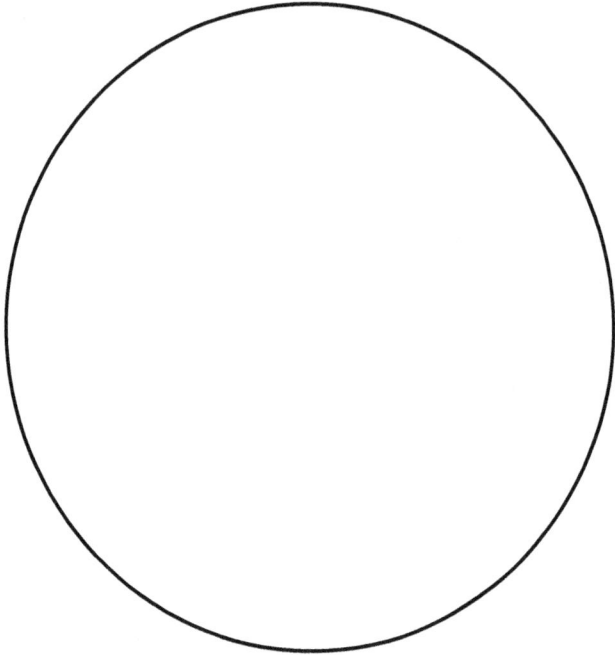

Apply your beliefs:

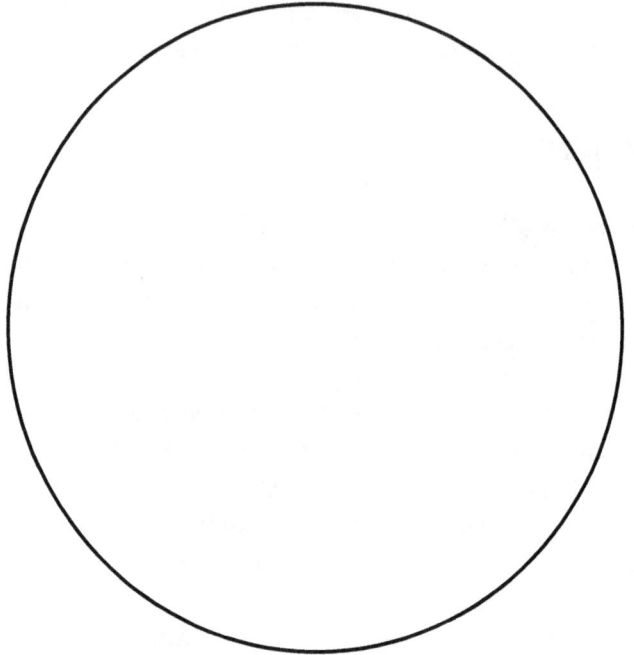

Apply best practices and research here:

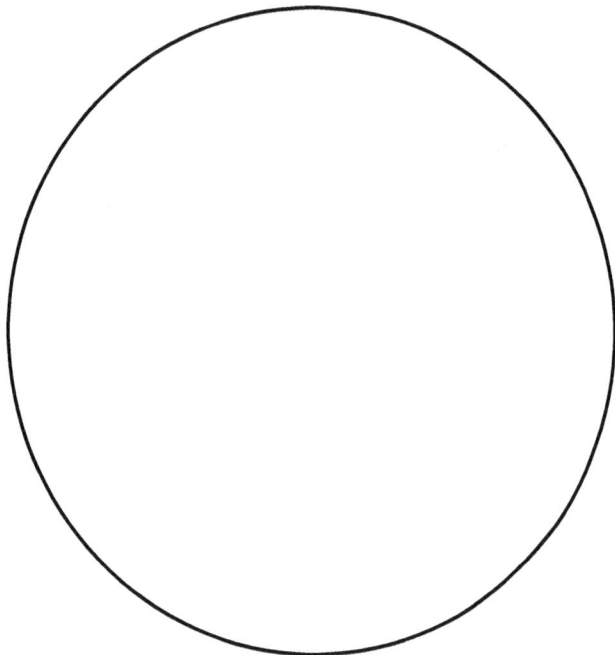

Apply your suggested interventions here:

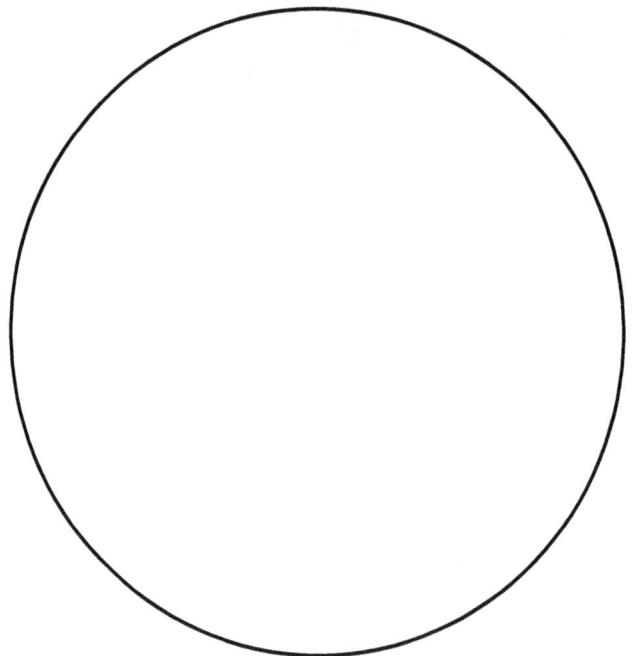

Processing: Case Study Reflection

What does "best practice" mean in how you would proceed with this client?

_____

_____

_____

_____

_____

_____

Identify your goals in working with this client, and indicate how you determined them.

_____

_____

_____

_____

_____

_____

_____

When have you used evidenced-based research this week?

What are some search engine words or phrases you can use to find research articles or other literature related to the work you want to do with Carlos?

_____

_____

_____

_____

_____

_____

What are best practices for work with Carlos (informed by your literature search)?

_____

_____

_____

_____

_____

_____

Describe some evidenced-based interventions (informed by your literature search) you might use with Carlos.

_____

_____

_____

_____

_____

_____

Taking It to the Group

- Have group members share their initial focus of Carlos. What beliefs do they hold about the client? How did they begin to conceptualize best practices for him?

- As a group, spend time reflecting on the process of research when examining this case. How do we use research? Specifically, what did literature provide in working with Carlos?

- What best practices and/or evidenced-based interventions for Carlos were identified by group members? What accounts for any differences that were found among the group members?

- What is some advice that the group might offer new counselors when beginning to incorporate literature and evidenced-based research into their counseling? How can peer supervision be valuable to counselors who are new to researching with the purpose of advancing their counseling methods?

- How can research support our advocacy efforts for the professional counseling field and for clients?

My additional thoughts and feelings about the
Case Study Reflection **activity...**

Supervisor Reflections

Follow-up Supervision Group Activities

- Based on group members' respective research and counseling knowledge, create a treatment plan for Carlos as a group.

- As a group, consider other ways to include evidence-based interventions and best practices in counseling. This might be related to clients, community programs, prevention, or even office set-up.

- Use research to inform your work as a supervision group. Investigate best practices in group supervision or a supervision intervention to implement together.

Activity 39: Job Assessment

Directions: Create an assessment form to evaluate potential job offers. Think of questions that would assess ways to identify aspects of job criteria and work environment that meet your needs. This is your original creation, and it can include anything that best represents your intention for evaluating a potential job.

Processing: Job Assessment

Describe how you approached this process. What is the intention of your assessment, and in what ways does it most reflect the things important to you when looking for a job?

_____

_____

_____

_____

_____

_____

How did you decide on questions related to job environment and job expectations or criteria?

_____

_____

_____

_____

_____

_____

When have you experienced the usefulness of assessment this week?

What did you learn about your future goals or your desires for a future workplace?

_____

_____

_____

_____

_____

_____

How did your knowledge of assessment, or things you learned in your related course, help you create your questions?

_____

_____

_____

_____

_____

_____

How can your own assessment process for a future job help you in making decisions?

_____

_____

_____

_____

_____

_____

Taking It to the Group

- Allow each group member to share their assessment. Encourage discussion on how they developed the assessment and what they used to help focus its development.

- As a group, consider some of the ways the assessments are used in the counseling field and how it may be beneficial to use these with clients.

- How does the group believe that assessment is related to counselor professional identity?

- What are some ways that peer supervision can be helpful with selecting, or creating, assessments to use with clients?

- Research has shown that assessments can wrongly identify issues with people. How can professional counselors use assessment in ways that reflect the shared philosophy of counseling?

My additional thoughts and feelings about the *Job Assessment* activity...

Supervisor Reflections

Follow-up Supervision Group Activities

- Exchange assessments with one another and complete each other's assessments using pretend job openings. Discuss the strengths and areas of improvement for the assessments and liken this process to what clients go through when they complete an assessment. What did group members learn that might make the assessment process go easier with clients?

- Create an assessment that reflects the groups' ideas of counselor professional identity.

- Bring in other assessments. Discuss the intention of the assessments along with reliability and validity. Spend time exploring the outcomes of the assessments.

Activity 40: Show and Tell

Directions: Remember show and tell at school? The idea was to bring something in that was meaningful to you and share with your class. This activity is all about showing and telling your classmates about you. Below are some questions that we want you to consider. Then bring in a small item that represents the answer. In all, you will have 10 items to bring to group.

1. Most important possession to you

2. Concern about entering the counseling field

3. Your clients'/students' description of you

4. One weakness you have

5. One strength you have

6. Your counseling style

7. What you want to be remembered for

8. Your preferred theoretical orientation

9. Proudest professional moment

10. Most impactful assignment

Processing: Show and Tell

What are some conclusions you can draw from your chosen items?

_____

_____

_____

_____

_____

_____

Evaluate your items and determine if this is an accurate interpretation of your counselor identity.

_____

_____

_____

_____

_____

_____

Choose one item from the list that describes the week you experienced.

If one of your items is not accurate, what could be a better representation of you?

_____

_____

_____

_____

_____

_____

What research and continued work do you need to do, as a result of your item selection, towards your counseling professional journey? For example, was it hard to select an item for a particular statement?

_____

_____

_____

_____

_____

_____

How could you use an intervention similar to this as a way to assess or evaluate the progress of your clients?

_____

_____

_____

_____

_____

_____

Taking It to the Group

- Have group members share their items for show and tell. Alternatively, instructors can organize the items without group members in the room. Then have members make guesses on which items belong to which group members.

- Provide group members with feedback about whether or not the item seems to match the group member.

- As a group, share the items that were hardest to select for the statements. Through assessment and evaluation, discuss if the item matched group members' intended message. For example, are members congruent with their inner and outer self?

- How can peers collaborate to ensure that counselors are congruent with how they are seen and how they want to be seen?

- How can you evaluate your progress with your clients? How is evaluation of the work we do with clients and the work we do with programs important to the longevity of counselor professional identity?

**My additional thoughts and feelings about the
Show and Tell activity...**

Supervisor Reflections

Follow-up Supervision Group Activities

- Have group members work in dyads, sharing more of their personal responses. This process can also incorporate practicing basic clinical skills.

- As a group, consider some of the ways the responses to the questions provide continued opportunities for growth and additional research.

- Complete this activity as a group. Select items that represent responses from the group's perspective.

References

American Counseling Association. (2014). *2014 Code of ethics.* Retrieved from www.counseling.org/resources/aca-code-of-ethics.pdf

Bardhoshi, G., Erford, B. T., Duncan, K., Dummett, B., Falco, M., Deferio, K., & Kraft, J. (2016). Choosing assessment instruments for posttraumatic stress disorder screening and outcome research. *Journal of Counseling & Development, 94,* 184–194. doi:10.1002/jcad.12075

Carey, J., Harrington, K., Martin, I., & Hoffman, D. (2012). A statewide evaluation of the outcomes of the implementation of ASCA National Model school counseling program in rural and suburban Nebraska high schools. *Professional School Counseling, 16,* 100–107.

Carey, J., Harrington, K., Martin, I., & Stevenson, D. (2012). A statewide evaluation of the outcomes of the implementation of ASCA National Model school counseling program in Utah high schools. *Professional School Counseling, 16,* 89–99.

Council for Accreditation of Counseling and Related Educational Programs. (2016). *CACREP accreditation standards and procedures manual.* Alexandria, VA: Author.

Erford, B. T., Jackson, J., Bardhoshi, G., Duncan, K., & Atalay, Z. (2018). Selecting suicide ideation assessment instruments: A meta-analytic review. *Measurement and Evaluation in Counseling and Development, 51,* 42–59. doi:10.1080/07481756.2017.1358062

Hayden, S. C. W. (2017). Fostering intentionality in career assessment through counseling supervision. *Career Planning and Adult Development Journal, 33*(4), 90–97.

Ibrahim, F. A., & Dykeman, C. (2011). Counseling Muslim Americans: Cultural and spiritual assessments. *Journal of Counseling & Development, 89,* 387–396. doi:10.1002/j.1556-6676.2011.tb02835.x

Jorgensen, M. F., & Duncan, K. (2015). A grounded theory of master's-level counselor research identity. *Counselor Education and Supervision, 54,* 17–31. doi:10.1002/j.1556-6978.2015.00067.x

Kaplan, D. M., & Gladding, S. T. (2011). A vision for the future of counseling: The 20/20 principles for unifying and strengthening the profession. *Journal of Counseling & Development, 89,* 367–372. doi:10.1002/j.1556-6678.2011.tb00101.x

Nielson, T. (2015). Practice-based research: Meeting the demands of program evaluation through the single-case design. *Journal of Mental Health Counseling, 37,* 364–376. doi:10.17744/mehc.37.4.07

Watson, J. C. (2012). Integrating assessment into the counseling process: Effective strategies for college counselors. *Journal of College Counseling, 15*(3), 195–197. doi:10.1002/j.2161-1882.2012.00015.x

CHAPTER 11

SELF-GROWTH AND THE FUTURE

The definition of self-growth has changed throughout the years and throughout different professions. There are multiple ways it can be defined. For this chapter, self-growth is the development of personal reflection, confidence, and compassion (Foss-Kelly & Protivnak, 2017). Self-growth involves awareness of oneself and the areas we need to improve upon. It takes it one step further and the awareness moves into action and change begins to take shape. Self-growth in the counseling profession is highly valued because it recognizes that, as people, we have areas to improve upon. The increase in our personal selves is most often translated into our work with clients. Hence, healthy counselors produce healthy clients (Lawson & Myers, 2011). Throughout the profession, self-growth has been found to be important to counselors evolving personally and professionally (Konstam et al., 2015).

Research indicates that the counseling profession values self-growth in order to help support counselors' sustainability in the field, and, in turn, their clients. The push to help counselor trainees to develop their understanding of self and to recognize areas of weakness or limitations is not new to the counseling profession. Often times this process is difficult and is a challenging part of academic training programs, yet self-growth has been found to be extremely valuable in helping counselor trainees become aware of what they need to improve to be the best version of themselves (Foss-Kelly & Protivnak, 2017). Wagner and Hill (2015) found that as counselor trainees first entered into academic counseling programs, fear, anxiety, and excitement existed. After experiencing the program and the personal and professional identity work that evolved over time, counselor trainees identified progressing into self-aware professionals. This work was connected to the efforts of self-growth and reflection.

The counseling profession has consistently supported the need for counselors to engage regularly in self-compassion as it can prevent counselor burnout and develop as a practitioner (Coaston, 2017). By employing more of these practices, it helps support wellness and self-awareness, which will only benefit clients and counselors. These concepts are integral to professional identity for counselors. Counselors are often looked at as a representative of success or normalcy. While this is not always the case, there are many counselors who are wounded healers with their own mental health struggles or diagnoses (Kern, 2014). Growth emphasizes the need for counselors to engage in self-exploration to sustain their career. It is important to integrate personal vulnerabilities and diagnoses with professional identity to achieve greater levels of authenticity and success in counseling. Reframing instances of imperfection and vulnerability is a way to grow as a counselor and achieve deeper understanding and empathy for clients. This enhances counselor professional identity and personal self-growth (Kern, 2014; Wolf, Thompson, Thompson, & Smith-Adcock, 2012). As counselors there is a responsibility to engage in reflection, which will lead to personal growth, a stronger professional identity, and a better outcome for clients (Pompeo & Levitt, 2014). It appears evident that there is a clear link between self-growth and self-awareness for the counselor on a personal level and positive professional outcomes for the clients. Burns and Cruikshanks (2017) also researched the value and need to clearly outline your professional identity to connect these elements together.

Foss-Kelly and Protivnak (2017) conducted an in-depth qualitative study to understand what counselor trainees need and valued in their academic programs. Most counselor trainees reflected on their own response to self-growth-oriented assignments, discussions, and mentored relationships that focused on these same themes. Often participants wanted faculty investment in student growth, the challenge of doing their own work, and experienced the value of working through some difficult experiences. These exercises that pushed their own personal boundaries to challenge their own beliefs and future goals were noted as most difficult to process, but crucial to understand what they need to work on moving forward. Smith and Koltz (2015) worked with school counselor trainees and their own experiences of personal growth. They conducted focus groups over a two-year period and several themes emerged, including personal growth. The research discussed how supervisors and faculty members can assist in supporting counselor trainees' movement towards self-growth and self-discovery, which can include preparations for future goals.

The counseling profession values the process of self-growth and continuously avoiding stagnation. As counselors, the commitment to care for yourself is well valued throughout the field. This, in turn, helps to determine areas that require further exploration and areas of limitations. The move towards the future reflects your personal goals, but it acknowledges your personal commitment to understanding the field of counseling and best practices for our clients. The field of counseling is always evolving and recognizes the constant change of needs for clients. The field has a variety of specialties and counselors may choose to focus on different areas as experts to support their own areas of interest, which positively impacts clients. By exploring your personal areas of self-growth, this may influence the areas in which you decide to develop expertise.

Connecting Self-Growth and the Future to You

Examining other areas of ourselves can enhance our ability to connect with our clients, which is of value to the counseling profession. Ultimately recognizing the areas that we need to work on can be thought of as cleansing our minds and hearts. When we work with clients and have a clear presence it helps us to connect to our clients and provide an environment of genuineness, warmth, compassion, and presence. The less we are dealing with ourselves, the more we are able to give to clients. It is important for counselors not to become fully enmeshed with clients, but our profession does involve giving our basic clinical skills and theoretical orientation to clients each and every session. There are times when our unfinished business blinds us or prevents us from the work we are required to do. This emphasizes the need of self-exploration and greater understanding.

The journey towards self-growth is a difficult process, most acknowledge it can be harder than learning theories and techniques because it forces each counselor to have to look inside and address all areas of the self. For many counselors it may mean facing some aspects of themselves that are not congruent with who they want to be, for others it may be processing experiences that they do not want to relive, or for others it be may a combination of experiences and personality traits. Regardless of what we need to examine in ourselves, we owe it to our clients to be the best version of ourselves. Importantly, we owe it to ourselves to be the best version we can be.

It can be difficult to push ourselves forward and continue to challenge ourselves to grow. Even though our profession has shown that there is value and need to continue to grow, there is a responsibility for each counselor to self-motivate. The activities in this chapter help to look at who you are, where you are going, and who you want to be. They each challenge you to examine your future and your movement towards achieving your goals. This may translate into becoming the best version of yourself. There will be difficult days with our clients and sometimes we need reminders on why we are in the profession. We can blur boundaries with client's stories, and in order to take care of ourselves, we need to learn to separate from our clients and have direction in our work. Much of the work we do helps to grow us further and helps promote who we are as professional counselors. At this stage in your professional identity, what you want to be known for and what you want to attain are important in identifying how to continue to grow yourself.

Activity 41: #PlayHardBeSmartHaveFun

Directions: There are so many opportunities and ways to create positive affirmations to help support our self-growth. These can be useful reminders to continue striving for more, being reflective, and continuing growth amidst experiencing difficulty or setbacks. They can also support our forward movement and keep us focused on our future self-growth plans. Create a series of messages/affirmations/hashtags that help maintain your current focus on self-growth and awareness, as well as movement toward becoming a professional counselor.

Text Message:

Hashtag:

Affirmation:

Motto:

Processing: #PlayHardBeSmartHaveFun

How does the theme of your messages reflect what you want for your future self-growth and ongoing awareness?

_____

_____

_____

_____

_____

_____

Which message do you believe will influence you the most?

_____

_____

_____

_____

_____

_____

When did you use your hashtag this week?

When will these messages be useful to you? Anticipate a time when you might want to use them and describe your hoped-for outcome.

_____

_____

_____

_____

_____

_____

Where could you display these messages so that when you are experiencing an obstacle they are readily available?

_____

_____

_____

_____

_____

_____

Could you use this technique with your clients? How would you encourage them to create their message?

_____

_____

_____

_____

_____

_____

Taking It to the Group

- Have each group member share the messages they created.

- Provide each other with feedback about how members' messages reflect traits and qualities that others have observed in them during the group supervision and self-growth process.

- How can these messages be used to shape your professional identity as a professional counselor? As a group, spend time discussing how an activity like this could be used with clients to help them shape their own future goals.

- What is some advice that the group might offer to new counselors regarding social media tools in their counseling practice and ways it can be used to help promote growth and awareness?

- How is ongoing self-reflection and awareness useful to counselor identity development?

My additional thoughts and feelings about the #PlayHardBeSmartHaveFun activity...

Supervisor Reflections

Follow-up Supervision Group Activities

- Have group members create their own hashtag for group supervision. It could be the creation of a group name that supports continued growth for the group.

- As a group, consider some of the ways setbacks will occur in the counseling field. How can the group prepare for setbacks and stay focused on self-growth and awareness?

- Have group members identify a quote that resonates with their journey to becoming a professional counselor and building a related identity. Share the quotes and consider posting in the group space.

Activity 42: To Whom It May Concern

Directions: Throughout this workbook you have done a lot of self-exploration and investigation about counseling professional identity. Think about what you have learned and consider how you envision demonstrating professional identity when you are a more experienced counselor. Though it will continue to evolve, think about a time in the future when you feel comfortable with your counselor professional identity and confident to demonstrate it to future generations of counselors. Imagine this future time in your life and write a letter to your current self from your future self (i.e., write a letter to the present from the perspective of you in 10, 15, 20, or more years). Provide yourself with insight into your identity development process and any challenges along the way, how you demonstrate your professional identity, words of wisdom, and anything else you think would be important.

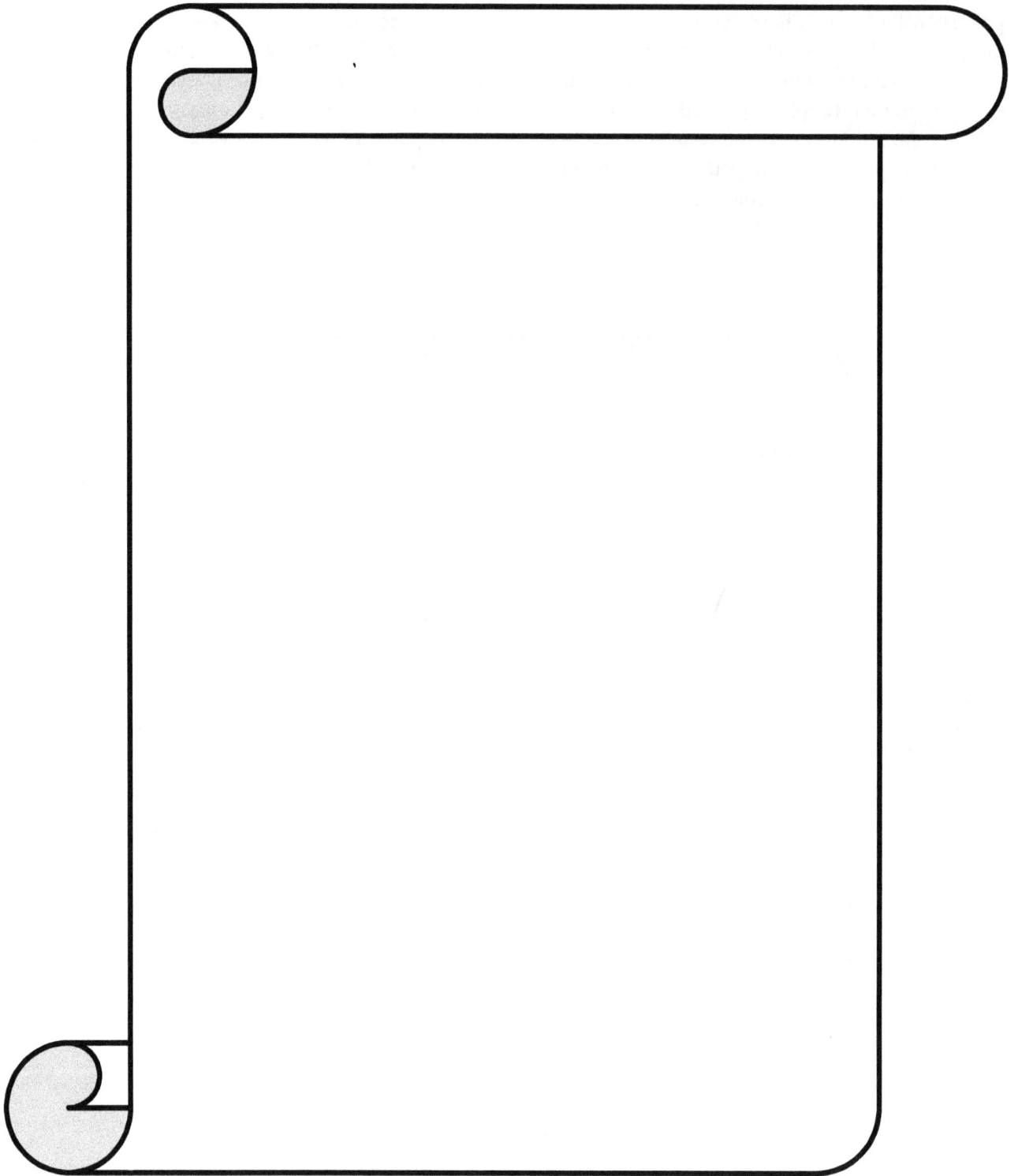

Processing: To Whom It May Concern

How do you remain open to self-growth and change?

_____

_____

_____

_____

_____

_____

What has influenced your ability to be reflective and open to change as you have learned more about yourself, professional counseling, and professional identity?

_____

_____

_____

_____

_____

_____

During what times has your growth and professional identity become evident to you this week?

What do you imagine will be the biggest contributing factor to your confidence in demonstrating and talking about counselor professional identity in the future? How will this factor influence you in this way?

_____

_____

_____

_____

_____

What value might there be in looking back over this letter in the future? How do you think it might change?

_____

_____

_____

_____

_____

How do you think you and your professional identity expression will change in the future?

_____

_____

_____

_____

_____

Taking It to the Group

- What are some common experiences group members had when looking back over what they have learned about counselor professional identity and applying it to the future?

- How were group members supportive during the process of self-growth? How can they continue to be supportive in the future?

- How have the group's ideas of professional identity evolved during its time together? What factors contributed to this evolution?

- Self-growth is something counselors facilitate in clients. How is it also essential to the development of a counselor?

- How does the group predict that the shared counseling professional identity will evolve in the future?

My additional thoughts and feelings about the *To Whom It May Concern* activity...

Supervisor Reflections

Follow-up Supervision Group Activities

- What do group members wish they would have known as they embarked on this journey of building a counselor professional identity? What would the group have done differently, or the same, if they could do it over?

- Write a Top 10 List of defining moments the group had in exploring self-growth and professional identity.

- Write a collective letter to an incoming group or new class of beginning counselor trainees to inform them about the counselor professional identity development journey they are embarking on. Provide them with a preview of what they might learn, advice, or information that the group wished it knew at the start of this process.

Activity 43: Color Code Your Future

Directions: Color is everywhere! Certain colors impact our mood and our mood impacts our color selection. Below is a list of colors. Think about the color and the connection it has to yourself. Identify what part of yourself is represented by that color and list a recent awareness you have had about yourself in this area. Then do the same process for your counselor professional identity development.

The Colors of You

Red _____

Orange _____

Yellow _____

Green _____

Blue _____

Purple _____

Brown _____

Black _____

White _____

Gray _____

The Colors of Your Counselor Professional Identity

Red _____

Orange _____

Yellow _____

Green _____

Blue _____

Purple _____

Brown _____

Black _____

White _____

Gray _____

Processing: Color Code Your Future

What color, and associated new awareness, was most prominent to you for each box?

_____

_____

_____

_____

_____

_____

If you were to consider something that overshadows or hides your counselor professional identity, what color would it be and what would it represent?

_____

_____

_____

_____

_____

_____

_____

Where have you experienced your "colors" this week?

How did your colors or aspects of your personal self and counselor professional identity match or overlap?

_____

_____

_____

_____

_____

_____

What areas of awareness are you most proud of? What areas of growth or awareness were easiest and why? What areas took more effort, and how?

_____

_____

_____

_____

_____

_____

How can you continue to make sure you are aware of your growth and development?

_____

_____

_____

_____

_____

_____

Taking It to the Group

- As a group, have group members share colors and connection to the different parts of themselves. Discuss any themes that may emerge among the group members' experiences with awareness and growth.

- Go around the group and share things group members have observed in others throughout the course of time together. These may be new awareness that members have of each other, ways they have witnessed peers' ongoing professional development, or changed perceptions.

- Discuss how awareness and self-growth are important for development of counselors. How, too, is it important for clients and how can professional counselors facilitate this process of bringing awareness to clients' behaviors, feelings, or thoughts?

- What advice might the group offer to an incoming practicum or internship group on how to continue self-growth?

- In what ways do leaders and counselors re-evaluate the profession, gain awareness about professional impact, and reflect on growth in order to strengthen and continue to evolve the field?

**My additional thoughts and feelings about the
Color Code Your Future activity...**

Supervisor Reflections

Follow-up Supervision Group Activities

- As a group, consider some of the ways to support self-awareness and self-growth. Discuss ways these two concepts can be directly connected to our emotions and thoughts about ourselves.

- Have group members create a rainbow with markers, crayons, or other items to represent the different parts of counselor professional identity or the shared philosophy of professional counseling.

- Create a group supervision color wheel describing who the group is and what they represent. Hang the color wheel as a group reminder.

Activity 44: Then, Now, Soon

Directions: Take photographs that represent three different time periods of your counselor professional identity. Take one photograph that represents the past by considering what you thought counseling and/or the role of a counselor was when you first started your counseling degree. Take a second photograph that represents your present professional identity. Finally, take a third photograph that represents what you hope your professional identity to be in five years.

Attach "then" photo here

Attach "now" photo here

Attach "soon" photo here

Processing: Then, Now, Soon

In what ways do your photos represent the corresponding time frame of your professional identity?

Then:

_____

_____

_____

_____

Now:

_____

_____

_____

_____

Soon:

_____

_____

_____

_____

When have you seen glimpses of your future professional identity this week?

What personal and professional attributes are evident in each time period of your professional identity?

_____

_____

_____

_____

_____

_____

What factors have influenced development from your "then" professional identity to your professional identity "now"?

_____

_____

_____

_____

_____

_____

_____

What did you think about and feel when taking your "soon" photograph? What will you do to attain this vision of your professional identity?

_____

_____

_____

_____

_____

_____

Taking It to the Group

- What themes from the professional identity photos and stories are among the supervision group? How are these themes evident in the shared vision and philosophy of counseling?

- In what ways has group supervision and the passage of time influenced the development of each member's professional identity?

- Identify the most helpful attributes group members offer to one another in an effort to nurture professional identity? Alternatively, what are qualities of the group that can be improved?

- What advice can the group offer to an incoming internship group regarding the beginning processes of developing a counselor professional identity?

- What steps will need to be taken in order to achieve a more developed counselor professional identity? How can the counseling profession be supportive and helpful in the endeavor of strengthening professional identity for its counselors?

My additional thoughts and feelings about the
Then, Now, Soon **activity...**

Supervisor Reflections

Follow-up Supervision Group Activities

- Title the photos to convey the meaning, feelings, and/or thoughts associated with the presented photographs.

- Define what it is to be a professional counselor and find one photo to represent that definition. Print and hang the photo in a visible place in your meeting room under a list of professional identity development goals that the group can strive for together.

- Choose a collective "soon" picture to represent the group's journey together toward counselor professional identity achievement.

References

Burns, S., & Cruikshanks, D. R. (2017). Evaluating independently licensed counselors' articulation of professional identity using structural coding. *Professional Counselor, 7*(2), 185–207. doi:10.1524/sb.7.2.185

Coaston, S. C. (2017). Self-care through self-compassion: A balm for burnout. *The Professional Counselor, 7*(3), 285–297. doi:10.15241/scc.7.3.285

Foss-Kelly, L. L., & Protivnak, J. J. (2017). Voices from the desks: Exploring student experiences in counselor education. *The Journal of Counselor Preparation and Supervision, 9*(2), 10–32. doi:org/10.7729/92.1181

Kern, E. O. (2014). The pathologized counselor: Effectively integrating vulnerability and professional identity. *Journal of Creativity in Mental Health, 9*(2), 304–316. doi:10.1080/15401383.2013.854189

Konstam, V., Cook, A. L., Tomek, S., Mahdavi, E., Gracia, R., & Bayne, A. H. (2015). What factors sustain professional growth among school counselors? *Journal of School Counseling, 13*(3), 1–40.

Lawson, G., & Myers, J. E. (2011). Wellness, professional quality of life, and career-sustaining behaviors: What keeps us well? *Journal of Counseling & Development, 89*(2), 163–171. doi:10.1002/j.1556-6678.2011.tb00074.x

Pompeo, A. M., & Levitt, D. H. (2014). A path of counselor self-awareness. *Counseling and Values, 59*(1), 80–94. doi:0.1002/j.2161.007x.2014.00043.x

Smith, A., & Koltz, R. L. (2015). Supervision of school counseling students: A focus on personal growth, wellness, and development. *Journal of School Counseling, 13*(2), 2–34.

Wagner, H. H., & Hill, N. R. (2015). Becoming counselors through growth and learning: The entry transition process. *Counselor Education and Supervision, 54*(3), 189–202. doi:10.1002/ceas.12013

Wolf, C. P., Thompson, I. A., Thompson, E. S., & Smith-Adcock, S. (2012). Wellness in counselor preparation: Promoting individual well-being. *Journal of Individual Psychology, 68*(2), 164–181. doi:10.1353/jip

EPILOGUE

Congratulations! You made it to the end of this workbook and have a culminating journal of your counselor professional identity development process. At the start of this book we told you that counselor professional identity is something that develops over time, but starts as soon as you begin professional counselor training. As an emerging, or new, counselor you are in the beginning stages of creating your own counselor professional identity. This identity is something that requires thought, and we hope the last 11 chapters and 44 activities contained in this book helped you with this reflective process.

Counselor professional identity is complex with many factors. The activities in the book focused on ideas gleaned from other writers and researchers who indicated that counselor professional identity development is the simultaneous process of becoming indoctrinated into the philosophical foundations and the greater community of the profession while intertwining personal identity with counseling skills, attributes, and beliefs (Auxier, Hughes, & Kline, 2003; Gibson, Dollarhide, & Moss, 2010; Moss, Gibson, & Dollarhide, 2014; Prosek & Hurt, 2014). As a result, over the course of this book you have had the opportunity to learn more about the philosophy and vision that unites professional counselors. You were also challenged to explore your motivations to seek a counseling career, as well as the beliefs, values, and experiences that are woven in your personal and professional identities. There were activities that focused on your personal and professional growth, helped you identify strengths and areas of further development, encouraged you to consider your needs for wellness and self-care, and prompted you to examine your sense of belonging via professional organizations. You also had opportunities to consider counseling competencies in unique and personal ways, such as connecting with theoretical orientations, pondering how your experiences influence ethical practice, using research and assessment for self-growth and awareness, and exploring cultural influences and biases on your work. All of these things had the common goal to help you feel confident in your understanding of what it means to be a professional counselor and lead you to the unique expression of your counselor professional identity.

We hope that all of the activities you completed and the notes and ideas you have written within this workbook can serve to be a memory journal and a resource for you to look back through in years to come. You might review this work to reconnect with your feelings as an emerging and new counselor when you are feeling discouraged. Perhaps, at different turning points or transitions in your career, you will come across this work and feel reminiscent of a time when your counselor professional identity was less developed and in its exploratory stages. Alternatively, you might never look at this workbook again but know that the reflections contained within were impactful in the moment. Nevertheless, the work you have completed took time and effort and the reflections may have catalyzed some thought and emotion to your beginning stages of counselor professional identity.

Though you completed the main activities in this book individually, they were processed within a larger group. It is our belief that counselor professional identity is built in community and through conversations with other professionals. As a result, you processed all of the activities with peers, discussed related points more in depth to hear multiple perspectives, and engaged in further group activities to continue to explore topics. By engaging with your group members, you might have solidified your beliefs about topics, evolved your thinking, or expanded your ideas further. As you listened to your peers' experiences and thoughts about certain topics, you might have felt strong emotions. Perhaps there were times when you felt closer to, or maybe further from, your peers. Regardless, you might have learned more about yourself, the profession, and the importance of discourse and relationship to build identities and communities. Looking into the future, you might run into some of your current peers at conferences or other work events and be reminded of how their influence over your counselor professional identity continues to resonate with you.

As a final activity to end this workbook, we want you to consider all you have gained throughout the time working individually and within a group on your emerging counselor professional identity. Reflect on what you have learned about yourself personally and professionally and how these things inform your identity and how you describe your work as a counselor to others. Spend time, too, reflecting on how your group members influenced your journey and the unique ways they impacted or taught you. This final activity asks you to provide feedback to your group members and share their influence over your counselor professional identity development. Further, this activity gives you the opportunity to summarize what you have learned about the profession and your place within it by giving you space to write your professional identity statement. Though professional identity development is ongoing, and you are in the beginning stages, you are fully equipped to write your own confident and strong statement of identity. Know, though, that in years to come this statement will evolve and strengthen with the experiences, interactions, and growth that are yet to come.

Activity 45: Termination Farewell Dinner

Directions: Termination can be difficult, but it is important to process experiences in group supervision when the time together comes to an end.

Imagine you are having a farewell dinner with your peers and supervisor. This dinner is to mark the end of supervision and your group experience together as you each worked on developing your respective counselor professional identities. Around the table is a chair for each group member. Label each chair with the name of the group member. Underneath or around the chair, write a note of what that person "brought to the table" in terms of the group's exploration of counselor professional identity development. Think about what they contributed and what they gave you. On the table, write what you believe you gave the group and contributed throughout your months together.

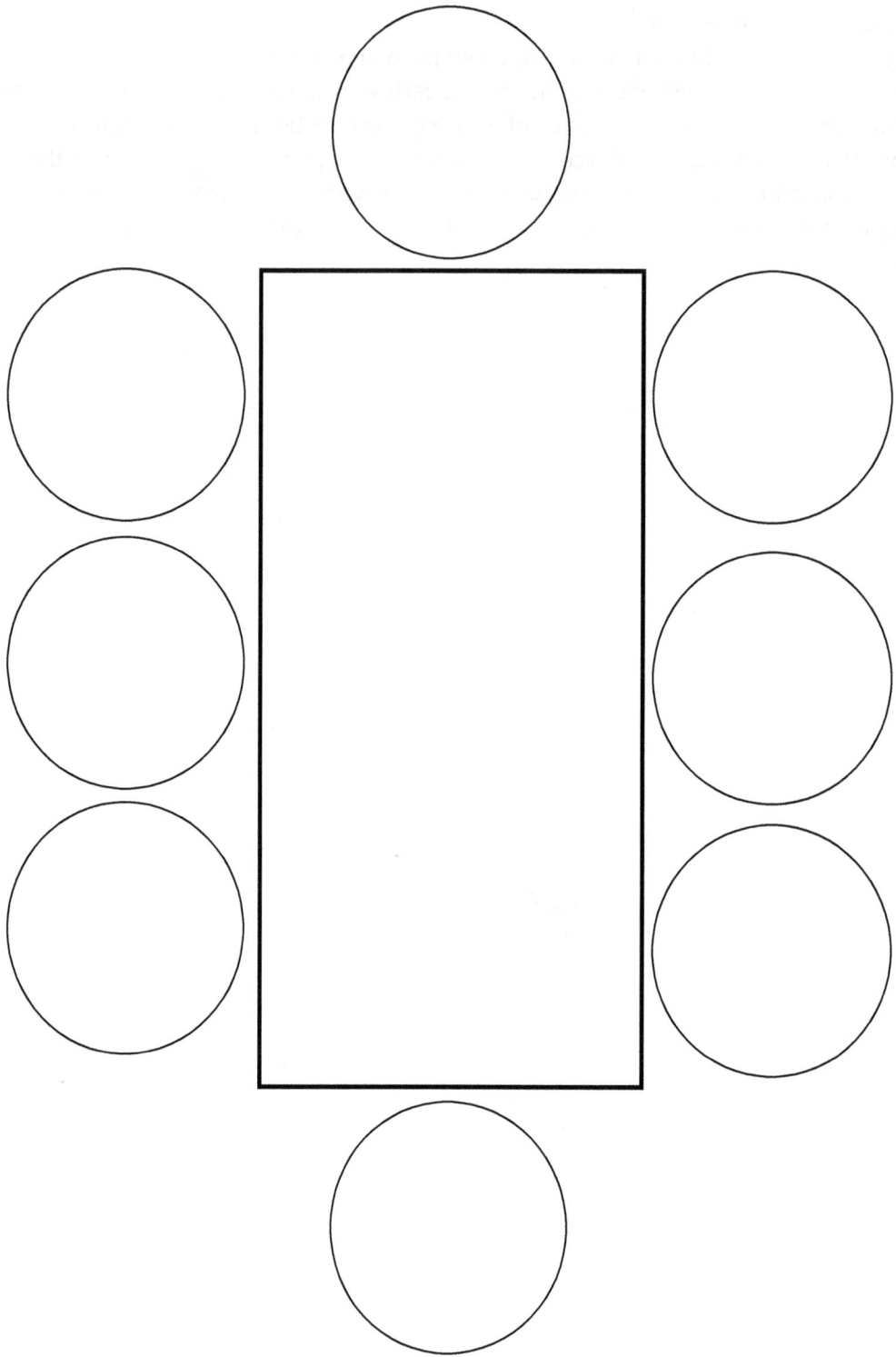

Processing: Termination Farewell Dinner

Which group member had the greatest impact on your counselor professional identity development?

_____

_____

_____

_____

_____

_____

Reflecting back, was there a specific group session that was most meaningful to you and your development?

_____

_____

_____

_____

_____

_____

Where did you hear the voices of your group members this week?

How will the group's work together continue to resonate with you and your future development?

_____

_____

_____

_____

_____

_____

How could you replicate this concept for terminating a counseling group in which you are the leader or supervisor?

_____

_____

_____

_____

_____

_____

_____

Reflecting on your group contribution, what would you change and what would you keep the same?

_____

_____

_____

_____

_____

_____

Taking It to the Group

- Have group members share what each member brought to the group. Allow for time so that each member can write down what is said about them (using the blank page at the end of the chapter).

- Discuss group members' responses to what others said about them. Is there something that surprised them? Is it what group members hoped they would contribute?

- As a group, spend time discussing how this could be used for clients in a group or family session. How could a format similar to this be used with your clients?

- What is some advice that the group might offer to an incoming practicum or internship group regarding the group experience and the benefit of peer supervision?

- Overall, how would the group define counselor professional identity and its importance for counselors and the professional counseling field?

My additional thoughts and feelings about the
***Termination Farewell Dinner* activity...**

Supervisor Reflections

Follow-up Supervision Group Activities

- What did the group bring to the table? What were the unique aspects of this group and how did it work together, as a system, to support members in professional identity development?

- Since each group member will have statements from members, discuss what members may do with this feedback. What is the impact of the statements on their professional identity development?

- Write a list of defining moments in the group's time together. List some implications from these moments that can help future counselors work on their own counselor professional identity development.

Reflections from Group Members

Each circle represents a group member. Identify the circle with the group members' name, then write what they shared about you. This will allow you to have this feedback as you continue on in your counseling journey.

Bonus Activity: Your Counselor Professional Identity Statement

Directions: Use the space below to write your professional identity statement.

_____

_____

_____

_____

_____

_____

_____

_____

_____

_____

_____

_____

_____

_____

_____

_____

_____

_____

_____

_____

_____

_____

_____

_____

_____

_____

_____

_____

References

Auxier, C. R., Hughes, F. R., & Kline, W. B. (2003). Identity development in counselors-in-training. *Counselor Education and Supervision, 43,* 25–38. doi:10.1002/j.1556-6978.2003.tb01827.x

Gibson, D. M., Dollarhide, C. T., & Moss, J. M. (2010). Professional identity development: A grounded theory of transformational tasks of new counselors. *Counselor Education and Supervision, 50,* 21–38. doi:10.1002/j.1556-6676.2014.00124.x

Moss, J. M., Gibson, D. M., & Dollarhide, C. T. (2014). Professional identity development: A grounded theory of transformational tasks of counselors. *Journal of Counseling & Development, 92,* 3–12. doi:10.1002/j.1556-6676.2014.00124.x

Prosek, E. A., & Hurt, K. M. (2014). Measuring professional identity development among counselor trainees. *Counselor Education and Supervision, 53,* 284–293. doi:10.1002/j.1556-6978.2014.00063.x

www.ingramcontent.com/pod-product-compliance
Lightning Source LLC
Chambersburg PA
CBHW080228270326
41926CB00020B/4181